NORTHERN LIGHT

JENPEG
SCHOOL
GR. 1
1977·8

NORTHERN LIGHT

Power, Land,
and the Memory of Water

KAZIM ALI

GOOSE LANE EDITIONS

Edited by Jim Schley and Rhonda Kronyk.
Front cover and page design by Mary Austin Speaker.
Cover photograph by Aaron Vincent Elkaim, featuring Jackson Osborne holding a photograph he made in Cross Lake in 1988, showing land that has since eroded. Copyright © 2016 by Aaron Vincent Elkaim.
Printed in the United States of America.
10 9 8 7 6 5 4 3 2 1

Published simultaneously in the United States of America by Milkweed Editions, 1011 Washington Avenue South, Suite 300, Minneapolis, Minnesota 55415. milkweed.org

Library and Archives Canada Cataloguing in Publication

Title: Northern light : power, land, and the memory of water / Kazim Ali.
Names: Ali, Kazim, 1971- author.
Description: Includes bibliographical references.
Identifiers: Canadiana (print) 20200302124 | Canadiana (ebook) 20200302094 | ISBN 9781773101989 (softcover) | ISBN 9781773101996 (EPUB) | ISBN 9781773102009 (Kindle)
Subjects: LCSH: Ali, Kazim, 1971-—Travel—Manitoba. | LCSH: Ali, Kazim, 1971-—Childhood and youth. | LCSH: Authors, American—Biography. | LCSH: Children of immigrants—Manitoba—Biography. | LCSH: Indigenous peoples—Manitoba—Social conditions. | LCSH: Hydroelectric power plants—Social aspects—Manitoba. | LCGFT: Autobiographies.
Classification: LCC PS3601.L375 Z46 2021 | DDC 818/.603—dc23

Goose Lane Editions is located on the traditional unceded territory of the Wəlastəkwiyik whose ancestors along with the Mi'kmaq and Peskotomuhkati Nations signed Peace and Friendship Treaties with the British Crown in the 1700s.

Goose Lane Editions acknowledges the generous financial support of the Government of Canada, the Canada Council for the Arts, and the Province of New Brunswick.

Goose Lane Editions
500 Beaverbrook Court, Suite 330
Fredericton, New Brunswick
CANADA E3B 5X4
gooselane.com

CONTENTS

NORTHERN LIGHT

1.

I'VE ALWAYS HAD a hard time answering the question "Where are you from?"

The easiest answer—the one I've fallen back on as a convenience, though I had always supposed it to be as true an answer as any—is that I am "from" nowhere. My father was born in India in Vellore, Tamil Nadu, and my mother in Hyderabad, then in Andhra Pradesh but now part of Telangana, but neither of them have formal birth certificates, only affidavits from neighbors attesting to their birth. As political refugees, both families had fled the increasing sectarian tension of Tamil Nadu of pre- and post-independence India. My mother's family had relocated to the then independent Muslim-ruled kingdom of Hyderabad in 1945, and during the Partition my father's family moved, along with hundreds of thousands of other Muslims, from South India to Karachi, at that time a mid-sized regional capital in the Sindh province, on the Arabian Sea. My father's later Pakistani citizenship has recently made it extremely difficult for me to travel in India because of new visa rules that prohibit people with Pakistani ancestry from being allowed to apply for multiple entry visas and that require them to apply for their visas not by mail but in person at a consulate. Those rules resulted from recent tensions arising from the victory of Hindu nationalist parties in national elections informed by a cultural movement known as *hindutva*, an ethnic absolutism that, among other things, promotes an erasure of Muslim influence on Indian history or

1

identity. So besides the daily alienation I feel growing, any average American or Canadian tourist has a far easier time visiting the cities of my parents' and grandparents' births and ancestries than I do. It is hard to feel like I am "from" a place that I have such limited access to, either culturally or physically.

My parents married in 1967 during a period of political and military conflict between India and Pakistan, a conflict that prevented my father from attending his own wedding. Ever a practical religion, Islam provides for marriage-by-proxy, and that is how the ceremony was performed. Unable to live together in either India or Pakistan, my parents, like many young Indian families, followed economic opportunity to London where my older sister and I were born; after a few years there and a brief return to Vellore, my family migrated to Canada in the early 1970s when Pierre Trudeau and the Canadian government were creating policies to encourage immigration. Siblings of both my parents, as well as their parents, soon followed. As if to imitate the spatial relationships of the shared living arrangements of the family complexes in Vellore and Hyderabad, my uncles and aunts moved to the same city, Winnipeg, in the province of Manitoba, and they lived in communal houses or had houses down the street or around the corner from one another. With their new Landed Immigrant cards from the Canadian government they were more officially documented in the new country than they ever had been in the old.

My younger sister was born in Winnipeg, but we didn't stay there long; after a year or two of living along the Red River, we moved north five hundred kilometers to a town that doesn't exist anymore. But even after we moved north, we continued to drive south for visits as often as my parents could. What I remember about those houses in Winnipeg at 23 Harmony Cove and 168 Sterling Avenue, at 317 and 106 River Road, at 10 St. Ann's Place where my extended family lived—the houses I visited throughout my childhood—is that the doors were always open. The screen doors would bang all day long with cousins running into the house to grab a snack and then out the door again, down Harmony Cove and up Sterling Avenue a hundred feet and into another door. Perhaps I was always a wanderer. No house claimed me. I could wake in one, eat in another, and bed down in yet a third.

So what does it mean to be "from" a place? What rights does this give you? For what status does a place of origin qualify a person? Am I from India or Pakistan? The ground shifted beneath our feet.

My father was an electrical engineer, working for Manitoba Hydro, the province's electrical power authority, and it was his job that took us north. Jenpeg was a small settlement of single and double trailers, built by Manitoba Hydro and perched on the banks of the Nelson River deep in the great boreal forests of the Canadian North. There were five residential streets named First, Second, Third, Fourth, and Fifth; a street with businesses on it (that we all perhaps optimistically, yet accurately, called "Downtown"); and a street simply called the Main Road running perpendicular and connecting the other six. When we first moved to Jenpeg, our family lived on Second Street, and then later when my father was promoted, we moved to another trailer on a little crescent off Main Road called—also optimistically—Nob Hill. At the time Jenpeg was several hours by car on dirt roads from Wabowden, the closest provincial town, northwest of Jenpeg, on the trunk road from Winnipeg to Thompson, a mining town even further north, where my uncle Ifteqar later moved with his family. Another town was even closer: Cross

3

Lake, on the Cross Lake Indian Reserve, but it was inaccessible by road from Jenpeg, except in the winter, when the lake had frozen over and you could drive across the ice.

It is of this isolated town, with its dirt roads and gravel driveways, that I have most of my earliest memories. It was there that I first attended school; there that I learned to read and write; there where I first looked up into the sky and asked my father questions about the designs I saw written there. Mine was, in many ways, an idyllic childhood. We stayed close to home: My sisters and our friends and I would play in our yards and the fields around town, warned by our parents to stay within sight of the buildings, since the woods that ringed us were home to bears, wolves, wolverines, moose, and other animals besides. In the winters we would snowshoe, or cross-country ski, or drag our toboggans to a slope behind the school and slide down into a hollow at the edge of the woods.

My father was there to work on the hydroelectric system of a generating station that would dam the Nelson River and provide power to Winnipeg and other cities to the south. That was an era of great projects. All across the Canadian north, the provinces were diverting local water systems into a few larger rivers and then damming those rivers. After extensive surveying of various rivers, Manitoba Hydro had identified the Nelson River, which flows from Lake Winnipeg north through the Cross Lake system and ultimately emptying into Hudson Bay, as an ideal site for a hydroelectric energy generating station. Some fifteen hundred workers and their families moved up into the forest where a clearing had been created, only a few kilometers from where the dam would be built. Single and double trailers were driven up to the site to create a town. The name "Jenpeg," according to the story I always heard in my childhood, came

4

from two women who worked in the Manitoba Hydro central offices in Winnipeg named Jenny and Peggy.

I had long wondered what became of the town I grew up in, with the tall green spruces seeming to brush against the often cloudy and low gray sky, the tepid summers, chilly autumns, and dark, thunderous winters. That landscape was the milieu of my childhood.

As far as I can remember we were the only nonwhite family in the town. Of the approximately four hundred people who lived there, about a hundred or so of us were children in the local school, which went from kindergarten to eighth grade. The kids who were high school age went to boarding school in Wabowden, coming home on the weekends. Of the five of us in my own immediate family, I may be the only one who still thinks about that place. When I asked my mother about what life was like there, she had to think about it a little. She said, "We were so young, we loved the people there." She told me about the friends she made among the other wives of the workers on the dam and about the minor battles she had with the school principal to get the teachers to work with me one on one because I was so bored in my classes. Still, when I told her I was trying to write about it, she was surprised, saying, "You know that we only lived there for a few years?"

But it doesn't feel like just few years to me—I suppose it wouldn't, not to a young child. And I don't remember being bored in my classes. In fact, I remember being thrilled to learn how to write my name in fat magic-markered letters from Miss Collins and to add and subtract from Mrs. Ruttle. One year in school we were supposed to make a booklet for each month of the year with a new picture for each day. I was so excited. As the month went on and the air got colder and the night came earlier, I started running out of ideas about what to draw. Nor, somehow, was I aware that months ended, so I kept going: September 31, September 32, September 33, September 34, September 35—I remember the date sharply—October 5— when the teacher finally got wise and had me backtrack and begin October on the right day. In some strange way, I still feel caught between time when I think of it, like I never really caught up. Maybe I never have.

One of the predominant sensory remembrances—I can still "feel" this in my body when I focus—is the cold. Already by Halloween there was snow on the ground, and we would have to hurry home from school as the sun's yellow darkened and darkened and the shadows stretched long. All winter the snow would pile up on the ground and the streets. I don't remember how the streets were cleared, but I do remember wearing a full-body zip-up snow suit to walk to school in the later months of the season.

And the sky: I remember the sky. More specifically, the night sky. In that small clearing in the forest, with no evening streetlights, the night was darker than any I have experienced since. On summer nights when the skies were cloud free and when the northern lights were not shining, making it difficult to discern the stars, we only had to stand outside for a few minutes for our eyes to adjust to the darkness, and a whole panoply of celestial light emerged. The constellations' names I learned made sense because the two Bears *looked* like bears, and I could easily see Orion the Hunter's right arm raising his club over his head, his left clutching a bow as he charged at Taurus the Bull.

My father had two telescopes, a refractor telescope he mounted on a tripod in the backyard and a larger, more powerful reflector telescope that he positioned on its base atop a table on the patio. The morning papers from Winnipeg would tell us what would be in the sky that night and where to look. My father, something of a genius at things mathematical, would take into account our higher latitudinal positioning, do some quick calculations in pencil on star-chart paper, and plot exactly where to point the telescopes to find our nightly quarry. We would look at planets, moons, stars, galaxies. I saw Jupiter through the telescope, and Arcturus, Betelgeuse, and the rings of Saturn. The poet in me was born then, as well: my father would tell us the stories of Perseus and of Andromeda, whose parents Cepheus and Cassiopeia bartered her life for the safety of their city—and then he would point out in the sky the constellations of the four characters. The night he told me the story of the Pleiades, he had me look up into the sky to see the cluster of six scintillating stars, and then showed me through the telescope that there were, in fact, seven main stars, the smallest huddling next to her sisters, with many more much smaller, unable to be seen with the naked eye.

We moved from Jenpeg in 1979, the summer before I started third grade. Our new home, on Staten Island, would be the furthest I could have imagined from that town in the woods. My new school, P.S. 22, had a thousand students riding buses from all over the island; the adjustment was not easy. Back in Manitoba, construction on the dam was completed in one more year, and the trailers were packed up and driven off the land: Jenpeg ceased to exist.

As the years went by, and one by one, my parents' brothers and sisters and their families moved from Manitoba to the Greater Toronto area, the forests of the north receded from my memory. From time to time I mused again on childhood days, but mostly those first winters of Jenpeg were replaced in my imagination and in my daily life by the equally snow-filled winters of western New York, where I mainly grew up after we left New York City, and later the winters of Ohio, where I lived for many years. It was in the middle of one such winter, in a drafty old Midwestern house in Oberlin with a polar vortex howling down through Canada to reach its icy grip around the southern shore of Lake Erie, that I began thinking again of the town where I grew up. Was the site still there? Was the dam still operational? I had no idea.

I typed the word "Jenpeg" into a search engine, but barely any results returned. The first few stories were just dry technical accounts of the generating station, which was indeed still in operation. There was no information at all about a town called Jenpeg. But then, further down the feed, I happened upon an article from several years earlier, entitled "Manitoba Hydro Evicted from Northern Dam Station." Evicted? I didn't understand. Didn't Manitoba Hydro own the land? Who was evicting them? And on whose land had I grown up?

I clicked on the news story to read further. The people from Cross Lake—who called themselves the Pimicikamak, but whom the Canadian government designates as "the Cross Lake Band"—under the leadership of their Chief, Cathy Merrick, had served Manitoba Hydro with eviction papers. Six hundred people traveled the twenty kilometers from Cross Lake to take custody of the generating station and adjoining housing complex, chaining shut the doors.

Merrick wrote of the 2014 occupation in a letter to the *Winnipeg Free Press*:

> *Manitoba Hydro has been a great benefit to the province as a whole. Hydro employs 6,500 people, provides inexpensive power, and has brought $5.2 billion into the province from exports of "clean" energy in the past decade.*

But for us "hydro" is a bitter word and "clean hydro" is an insult. Our homeland has been ruined, the promises of fair treatment have been ignored and to add insult to injury, literally, our hydro bills are much higher than the provincial average.

Imagine if the once-pristine waters in the lake by your cottage became murky and the shoreline continually washed away. Imagine your favourite childhood camping sites eroded right off the map, your industries undercut, your favourite golf course denuded, your ancestors' graves dug up, and your place of worship defiled. Imagine if you had to constantly fight for compensation and mitigation, while paying monthly bills to the victimizer.

Despite all the damage we suffer, our community collectively pays Hydro about $3.6 million annually in hydro bills. Every bill is a reminder of the indignity done to us. Then, after contributing to our poverty, Hydro disconnects our people when they can't pay.

Chief Merrick went on to contend that Manitoba Hydro, the province of Manitoba, and the federal government of Canada had not fulfilled their agreements in the Northern Flood Agreement (NFA), the 1977 treaty with five northern Bands under which Manitoba Hydro received easement rights to build the generating station.

The town where I had grown up was on unceded land.

As I came to learn, since unrecorded time that land, and the people on it, had been called Pimicikamak, meaning "where a lake lies across the river"—a fairly accurate description of the hydrogeography of Cross Lake: the Nelson River flows into the eponymous lake and then continues out

9

of the lake on its journey north to the bay. Pimicikamak land spanned the northern region above Lake Winnipeg and Lake Winnipegosis, stretching across what are now the Canadian provincial borders of Saskatchewan to the west and Ontario to the east. The people of the region first encountered Europeans in the form of English traders who had been offered rights to trade in the region of Hudson Bay by the English Crown and the French traders who rushed in to compete with them when New France collapsed. A register book of an English trading post dating to 1770 lists the "Pemmichi-ke-me-u" among the various Indigenous communities who came to trade, and archeological evidence reveals the presence of Indigenous communities in that region of northern Manitoba for many more thousands of years.

With the "Royal Proclamation of 1763," England positioned its North American colonies in a nation-to-nation relationship with what it claimed to recognize as independent sovereign states. The proclamation was designed to ensure that only the Crown could control how quickly and in what manner Indigenous lands were settled; it recognized that "Great Frauds and Abuses have been committed in purchasing lands of the Indians, to the great Prejudice of our Interest and to the great Dissatisfaction of the said Indians." The proclamation forbade settlers from taking Indigenous land without the express permission of the Crown. For the next hundred years, these commonwealth colonies of Canada maintained an ostensibly equitable political relationship with the Inuit and other Indigenous Peoples of the region, though throughout this time economic rivalry over control of the fur trade and overt military conflicts between England and France, often involving rival Indigenous communities, coupled with the devastating impacts upon the Indigenous communities of European diseases and the introduction of high-proof alcohol as part of trading negotiations, undermined the philosophical principle of the proclamation by destabilizing Indigenous communities. Many communities were restricted onto smaller and smaller portions of land, often at a distance from their traditional territories. Both France and England also encouraged missionary activity designed to assimilate Indigenous populations into the religious and cultural practices of the European settlers.

In 1867, England's Parliament passed the British North America Act (now known as the Constitution Act), creating the Federal Dominion of Canada, comprised of what is now southern Ontario, Nova Scotia, and New Brunswick. In addition to formalizing the Dominion of Canada, the Act gave the new Canadian government the mandate and right to create legislation and govern the Indigenous Peoples and their lands on behalf of the British Crown. It also made the federal government responsible, rather than provinces or localities, for providing Indigenous Peoples with all the services that are normally provided by provincial governments, such as education and health care, fiduciary responsibilities that continue to this day. Included in this act were formulae for qualifying who counted as "Indigenous" in the first place; these were, firstly, "men of Indian blood reported to belong to a Band"; secondly, their children; and finally, "their spouses." Many of the northern Cree cultures were then—and still are—matriarchal, so this legal composition, centered on men as the point through which any woman had legal standing, was culturally destabilizing and willfully discounted traditional Indigenous family structures.

The law's intention was to empower agents of the Crown to treat with the northern communities around resource sharing and extraction, land tenancy for European settlers, and

11

transit rights through the arduous forests and rivers of "frontier" territories. By 1869, the Canadian government had passed another law annexing what was formerly called Rupert's Land—the territory surrounding Hudson Bay and James Bay—the Northwest Territories and the Arctic Islands—and set about negotiating a series of numbered treaties with the Métis, the Cree, and the Inuit. The first seven of these treaties, covering southern and central portions of Ontario, Manitoba, Saskatchewan, and Alberta, were negotiated between 1871 and 1877. About twenty years later, once the north had been opened to settlement and the Canadian settlers realized the full and rich resource potential of its timber, minerals, and northerly water access, four more treaties were negotiated by Canada with Inuit and sub-Arctic communities.

Pimicikamak territory was cartographically surveyed and added to the provisions of Treaty 5, which had been signed between the government, the Salteaux, and the Swampy Cree. When Pimicikamak was added to the treaty in 1875, it was provisionally agreed to by the leader of the Pimicikamak delegation, Tepastenam, a Medicine Man or "conjurer," as he was described in the records of Alexander Morris, the Crown Representative. For his part, Tepastenam, who was not a Chief, but attending the meeting as the official delegate from his people, anticipated he would be able to consult with his community and continue the conversation with Crown representatives the following year. The Canadian land agents, on the other hand, codified the 1875 agreement and demanded that the Pimicikamak honor the proposed demarcation, which—having little choice in the matter—they did. While on the surface of it—like the Royal Proclamation of 1763—the treaty appeared to be a gesture toward a certain kind of equitable political relationship, its true intent was to open northern

Manitoba to settlement and resource extraction and begin to erode Indigenous title to northern lands. The numbered treaties also designated the various traditional Indigenous communities into "Bands," hence the Pimicikamak became known to the federal government as the Cross Lake Band. Tepastenam was elected as the Cross Lake Band's Chief and served in that capacity until his death in 1881.

The Jenpeg Generating Station, the Nelson River that it spans, and the old town of Jenpeg where my family lived all lie inside the land that was recognized by the Crown as Pimicikamak sovereign territory in Treaty 5, called the Cross Lake Indian Reserve by the government of Canada. Chief Cathy Merrick and the people of Pimicikamak were litigating Manitoba Hydro's presence on what they have always considered—and still do consider—to be their own sovereign territory: sacred, never ceded, and only leased under previously agreed-upon terms to Manitoba Hydro, the province of Manitoba, and the Government of Canada.

In fact, as Chief Merrick explained in the letter published in the *Winnipeg Free Press*, the 2014 occupation of the Jenpeg Generating Station was the latest in an ongoing series of protests and litigation against the 1977 Northern Flood Agreement, and the latest demonstration of Indigenous resistance to a history of oppression by the government of Canada.

After the Canadian government had negotiated the first of the numbered treaties in the 1870s, they set into action an array of new laws that restricted the sovereignty and political rights of Indigenous Peoples, including the Indian Act of 1876. Not only were the provinces granted the right to expropriate portions of the Native reserves for public works, an allowance that remained in place until 1985, but in 1911 they also instituted a rule permitting the government to relocate any reserve located near a Canadian town of eight thousand or more residents. These relocations could be done without consultation or approval of reserve residents. The Squamish Nation sued the provincial government of British Columbia to overturn this law in 1977, after they were relocated; the federal Canadian court system did not definitively overturn the law and award the Squamish compensation until 2002.

However, the greatest damage done in Canada under the Indian Act was the active separation of Indigenous Peoples from their own languages and cultures. Not only were the original and ancient traditional nations re-categorized into the legal designation of "bands," with names given to them by Canadian officials, but the Indian Register also renamed the citizens of the bands with European-style names, in some cases given by government agents who traveled to the reserves and simply assigned their own family names to Indigenous individuals and families. Because of this, no relationship is assured when Indigenous Peoples in Canada share a surname, other than that their ancestors may have been named by the same agent. Traditional ceremonies—for example the Sun Dance, a ceremony of the Plains Cree—were outlawed. Commerce, including the selling of agricultural produce, was prohibitively restrictive. The new restrictions on selling agricultural produce and other products off-reserve were intended to create an agricultural monopoly for the farms of European settlers, and was compounded by the institution of a pass system, hindering travel. Most egregiously, in 1886 the government created and funded the residential (or "boarding") school system designed, in words attributed to one of its architects, poet Duncan Campbell Scott, "to kill the Indian in the child."

Confronted with the new political and economic realities of restriction on free passage and trade, many of the bands agreed to send their children to the residential schools because they wanted them to be educated in Canadian customs, to learn English, and to study math, western science, and other subjects. They believed this would give their children the best possible future. By 1920 attendance in the residential schools became compulsory for all Indigenous children between the ages of six and sixteen. Besides the trauma of family separation, the children were not permitted to speak their native languages and corporal punishment and sexual abuse by school staff were rampant and eventually well documented. To add insult to injury, annuities due to children under the numbered treaties were often redirected to the budgets of the schools themselves.

Some in the Canadian medical profession recognized the public health disaster posed by the residential school system early on. Peter Bryce, a government physician, documented the high incidence of tuberculosis and influenza in his 1907 "Report on the Indian Schools of Manitoba and the Northwest Territories," but his recommendations for containment and treatment were rejected, and the government subsequently withdrew funding for Bryce's research.

The residential schools also carried out extreme medical testing and nutritional experiments on students. This experimentation on human subjects was happening in Canada, as investigative journalist Tanya Talaga has pointed out, during the well-publicized Nuremberg Trials of Nazi war criminals including doctors—tribunals that raised issues and arguments around medical ethics. Even after the 1947 judgment against Nazi medical experimentation (commonly called the "Nuremberg Code"), Canadian physicians were experimenting with Indigenous children, withholding riboflavin, thiamin, and other essential nutrients to study the impact of malnutrition, even while the children sickened and died, and in some

15

experiments intentionally starving children to death to monitor the progress of the effects of starvation. The trauma wrought by the residential school system was multi-generational and resulted in loss of language and family structures. It is notable that although in 2008 Canadian Prime Minister Stephen Harper formally apologized for the residential school system, among all member states of the United Nations only Canada, New Zealand, Australia, and the United States did not sign the 2007 Declaration on the Rights of Indigenous Peoples. While New Zealand and Australia signed in 2009, and the United States the following year, Canada did not sign until 2016, and it was not until 2018 that this signing was affirmed by the House of Commons.

It feels obvious to say that the residential school system that existed in Canada—like the system of Indian boarding schools in the United States—existed so that young people taken from their families would be raised apart from their traditional lands in an effort to break cultural, linguistic, and political bonds between Indigenous Peoples and their communities. The social problems exacerbated by these generations of family separation—substance abuse, interfamily violence, and the loss of language and cultural heritage—continue to this day.

The last residential school in Canada did not close its doors until 1996.

*

As the polar vortex receded from Ohio, Jenpeg and Cross Lake remained on my mind. I couldn't stop thinking about the landscapes of my childhood. I would wake up in the night, thinking of the deep cold lake that had gathered near the shores of Jenpeg as the river swelled at the dammed point.

What was happening there *now?* I wanted to know. Sitting at my computer in the twilight hours before the cold winter sun dawned, rather than search for "Jenpeg" I typed "Cross Lake." Dozens of stories unrolled. I slumped back in my chair, reading a story I could never have imagined.

Just a year before, in the winter, six young people in Cross Lake between the ages of fifteen and eighteen had died by suicide in the space of two months, and in the weeks that followed there were at least one hundred and forty cases of attempted suicide by people under the age of twenty-five. Hundreds more young people under the age of twenty-five were placed on a suicide watch list.

What on earth had happened?

I read further, but the more I read, the less sense it made. One hundred and forty suicide attempts in a community of six thousand people, with no resident mental health counselor or therapist? The Pimicikamak had declared a mental health emergency and were requesting aid from the provincial and federal governments. The Elders in the community had gathered and performed a sacred ceremony calling on the spirits of the land and water to assist.

I couldn't believe what I was reading.

Tanya Talaga draws a direct connection between the residential school system and the current crisis in Indigenous communities around substance abuse, mental health, and wellness. For the period she studied, Talaga recounts that there were 126 suicides per 100,000 men compared to 24 suicides per 100,000 for non-Indigenous men. The numbers for women are as grave: First Nations women died by suicide at a rate of 35 women per 100,000, whereas the number of non-Indigenous women dying by suicide in the same period was 5 per 100,000. For the Inuit communities of the sub-Arctic and Arctic regions in Canada, the numbers are shockingly higher: Inuit young people aged fifteen to twenty-four in the period Talaga studied died by suicide at ten times the national average. The data she examined from other colonized populations around the world, including the Sámi in Finland and Indigenous populations in Brazil, were comparable. From the Pacific Islands to Palestine, to this day one can see that the sociopolitical impacts of colonialism such as land dispossession, cultural assimilation, disruption of traditional economies, and political disenfranchisement are accompanied by crises in the mental and spiritual well-being of the colonized communities.

In discussing the sexual abuse that occurred in the residential schools, Talaga describes a chain of impacts that continue to ripple outward, and the difficulties of recovering from that trauma: "In the absence of any wide-scale mental health and wellness system, the onus is on the survivor, or the child or the grandchild of the survivor, to find their way back."

My mind was racing. I had to know more about what was happening in Cross Lake, so I wrote to the only e-mail address I could find on the internet—Chief Cathy Merrick's. I told her that I was a writer and that I had grown up in Jenpeg. I told her my father had worked for Manitoba Hydro and then I asked her a few basic questions about the situation in Cross Lake. I asked her if she could point me in the direction of any news articles or research materials that might help me learn more about the community's activism around the Jenpeg Generating Station. Several days passed before I received a brief email in response: "It is wonderful that you would reflect on your childhood. . . . You are more than welcome to visit our Nation."

I stared at the screen. No answers to my questions, but an invitation to come and visit? There? Go back north after all these years? I wouldn't even know how to get there. All I remembered from my childhood were the grueling car trips we took, the hours on the dirt roads and provincial highways. My mother and father would wake my sisters and me before sunrise and transport us in our pajamas to the sleeping bags already laid out in the back of my father's humungous Mercury Montego station wagon, made even roomier by putting the back seats down. Even leaving at three or four in the morning, it would take us until early afternoon to arrive, screaming with glee, at 23 Harmony Cove in Winnipeg where my two youngest uncles lived along with my maternal grandparents, Zahra and Sajjad Sayeed. The one time we flew directly to Jenpeg from Winnipeg was when we first moved there. It had been a small six-seat propeller plane, and all I really remember about the trip were the incredible noise of the engine and how sick I was, the whole way there and for days after.

Go back north? When the place I really wanted to go— the town of Jenpeg—apparently didn't exist anymore? And yet the possibility of seeing Cross Lake haunted me. What had happened there was somehow a part of me, too.

There was some irony in my surprise at learning about what had happened and about my sudden hesitation at making the trip. I was no stranger to challenging travel. I'd spent years traveling to the Palestinian territory in the West Bank, teaching yoga and training yoga teachers in Ramallah. I'd seen the impacts of occupation and political disenfranchisement up close. I had seen the impact the checkpoints had on free passage and on the economic and social conditions of the Palestinians. Working with actual physical bodies in the yoga practice even taught me the kinds of mental and physical trauma individual people can manifest when the culture and history of a people are threatened. What made it possible for me to recognize the damage that colonialism far from home had wrought when I'd thought so little about damage that I myself might have played a role in?

And why was Jenpeg suddenly on my mind? How is it that all these years had passed and I had never once thought of Cross Lake, but suddenly here I was e-mailing with the community's Chief? In the days that followed my course became more and more clear to me, more and more real, more and more inevitable. I explored travel options. I bought plane tickets.

I was going back. I was returning north.

2.

CHIEF CATHY MERRICK put me in touch with David "Lee Roy" Muswaggon, one of the members of the executive council who was responsible for monitoring the implementation of the Northern Flood Agreement, the comprehensive treaty co-signed in 1975 by the provincial government, the federal government of Canada, Manitoba Hydro, and the five northern First Nations that would be affected by the building of the dam, including the Pimicikamak.

The actual Jenpeg Generating Station is a place I remember only a little bit, having visited the structure while it was under construction and when the river was flowing freely through. This dam was a joint project between the Canadian government and the government of the USSR and is one of very few examples of Soviet engineering still in active use in North America. Growing up, we knew Russian families who lived in Jenpeg, and two Russian boys were in my class at school. The Russian families all lived on Fifth Street next to one another, and it was rumored that a representative of the Soviet government was living in Jenpeg with them as a chaperone of sorts. One of the older Russian gentlemen resembled my paternal grandfather, and so, to help assuage my little sister's homesickness for the family, he would often come to our trailer and play with her, pretending to be him. She would call him "Ava," which is what we called our grandfather. I am not sure she ever realized that the old Russian gentleman wasn't our grandfather, even though Ava himself also came to visit the family while we lived there.

I gave Lee Roy a call. "So you want to come back to Cross Lake?" he asked me, sounding a little skeptical, I thought.

"Well, I'm not sure if 'back' is right, because in all the years I was growing up in Jenpeg, I never came to Cross Lake."

"Is that right?" he asked slowly. He sounded distracted to me, as if he was engaged in another task while speaking with me.

I started getting nervous. "Well, you know my mom and her friends used to drive over the lake in winter to shop, buy moccasins and gloves and that kind of thing."

There was a pause on the other end of the line. Lee Roy was shifting papers around, saying something to someone. "So why do you want to come back now?" he asked.

I wasn't sure if his apparent wariness was because he didn't trust me, or how much Chief Merrick had told him.

"Well, I grew up in Jenpeg," I said, "and my father was one of the engineers on the dam, but I never really knew what happened there. I want to see for myself the environmental damage and learn about the social and economic impact of the dam on Cross Lake."

Lee Roy was silent. I took it not as skepticism now, but rather a conversational pattern I would come to know better in the coming weeks—silence as an invitation, silence as interest.

"You know," I said then, awkwardly trying to make a connection, "I've visited Israel, I've been to the West Bank. I spent a lot of time learning about the issues that face the Palestinian people who live in the countryside and the villages—the ways the occupation has impacted them in their daily lives, impacted their families."

"Is that right?" Lee Roy asked again.

Buoyed by what I perceived as more interest in his tone, I continued, "Well, their traditional agricultural techniques rely on desert-sustainable water practices, but most of the Israeli

22

settlements in the West Bank are placed directly on top of the main aquifers, which they pipe back into treatment centers in Israel, so the Palestinians have to buy back the water, and their allotment is not always sufficient."

Lee Roy was silent. Not uninterested. Listening.

"I want to visit Jenpeg," I blurted out. "I mean the old town site, yes, but I need to know about Cross Lake as well. I don't think I can understand my childhood until I know what happened in your community."

I wasn't sure if I was explaining myself well enough. The truth is, I'm not sure I myself knew the reasons for my trip well enough to explain them to him.

"All right," said Lee Roy then, perhaps convinced by my clumsy entrée. "Can you come on Saturday evening? I want to invite you to take part in a Sweat Lodge ceremony. After you go through that, we will show you everything there is to show you here and answer all of your questions."

"A Sweat Lodge?" I asked, a little surprised.

"It's one of our most sacred ceremonies," he said. "We want to make sure you know this isn't about political power or money for us; it's about the soil, the rocks, the river. They are our Mother, and our life doesn't feel right without her. We want to share with you something of what we are, first. Then we can talk to you about the treaties, about the dam."

I hung up with Lee Roy, newly uneasy. What was I getting myself into? I had had some strange, nostalgic idea about going back to the town of my childhood, trooping through the forest on whatever access road I could find, and then maybe writing some dizzy remembrance about the trees and the water. And now I had agreed to be a part of some kind of ceremony in a community I barely knew. Would I be going there as a poet or as a journalist? An ethnographer or scholar or memoirist?

23

Or just a lonely person who wanted to look at a place he once
thought of as home?

I was acutely aware that each of those roles has its own
array of ethical considerations, and I felt prepared for none of
them.

*

Just before leaving for Manitoba I went to a poetry festival in
Salem, Massachusetts. I spent three days there among poets
and writers, understanding who I was and what I was supposed to do. I remembered a time twenty years earlier when
I'd been at the Dodge Poetry Festival in New Jersey. Three
friends from graduate school had driven out with me from
New York City and we were all staying in a motel room together down the road from the festival. The day I remember
most clearly from that time, I was attending a panel on the
responsibility of poets to engage political affairs. The three
poets on the panel were Yusef Komunyakaa, Anne Waldman,
and Nellie Wong. Komunyakaa claimed that artists ought to
have no political agenda or goal in their work but bring all
of their sensibilities to bear on the writing. Certainly, as the
author of many acclaimed books of poetry, including some
relating to American military involvement in Vietnam, this
approach had yielded great artistic achievement on his part.
Wong expressed the view that political and social realities
come first and foremost and are an integral part of the
writer's life; in her case, the organizing and political actions
she was involved in had become the subjects of her work.
Anne Waldman said what I thought to be the most interest-
ing thing, which was that artistic practice is itself political
action. She argued that the making of art could effect real

24

and lasting social change in the lived world. The thought comforts and unsettles at once.

Twenty years later, on the last day of the festival in Salem, I stopped at one of the tables in the book fair where a young woman was folding tiny origami cranes. She aimed to fold a thousand of them throughout the festival. She invited people to sit with her at the table and learn how to fold cranes; these were then collected in trays for people to take home. I chose an orange crane and put it in the pocket of my jacket.

That night, at the hotel, I called my friend Layli Long Soldier and told her about my upcoming trip to Cross Lake. Layli is like me, somewhat of a wanderer, having been raised in the Southwest—living in the Phoenix Valley as a child, in the Four Corners area as a teen, then on the Navajo Nation and in Santa Fe, where she lives now. She also has family on the Lakota reservation, whom she often visits. Layli's book of poetry *Whereas* has played a huge role in how I understand the actively moving parts of Indigenous language and existence on the North American continent. Her work tries to excavate sediments of hidden history, language, and politics, and I felt a sense of kinship with her as I wondered to myself, what would I discover in Cross Lake? I needed to talk to her.

"Kazim!" she exclaimed, when I explained to her what was going on, that I was leaving for Manitoba the next morning. "I never knew this about your childhood, that you grew up on the rez!"

I laughed. "I never knew either. No one told us we were on treaty land. I didn't know anything about Cross Lake except that's where the *other* kind of Indians lived."

"That's always the secret," said Layli. "Whose land you are on, what happened there before."

"In fact," I said, "when we were little, we didn't even think about the people in Cross Lake. I kind of vaguely remember people saying things about them, not really kind things. Stereotypical stuff."

Layli was silent.

"Am I betraying my father somehow by going?" I asked her bluntly. "Even though honestly, I'm sure he had no idea about what might happen because of the environmental impact of the dam. How was he supposed to know? And who knew the province would screw up the treaty promises?"

"I think you're honoring him by going," Layli said then. "You're going to represent him and to help remediate in some small way."

"Do you think?" I said. "But I don't know. What can I really do? Write about it? How's that going to matter? Who's going to read what a poet has to say?"

"Well," she said matter-of-factly, "you can't avoid it anymore. You opened the door. Why are you *really* nervous?"

"Do you think the people there are mad at me or my father?" I ask.

She pauses. "They wouldn't ask you to sweat, if that were the case," she says.

"Maybe. I'm wondering what they are expecting of me, though," I replied. "I'm going up there and I'm going through this Sweat Lodge—are they trying to purify me or something?"

"That isn't how it works," Layli said. "Our spirituality isn't transactional. It's an invitation to you to share in their life. They are welcoming you as family. They are inviting you into their community and their sacred space. There are no strings attached to that from their side, because they believe in the powers of the ceremony itself. But don't go in if you aren't willing to be changed."

I *wasn't* sure. If anything, I felt apprehensive. My father is one of the men who built this dam that led to so many broken promises, to such economic, social, and environmental disaster. How could I account for that?

"People have been connected to the land for thousands and thousands of years," Layli continued. "To be cut off from it is not a small thing; but honestly, Kazim, when you think about how few years it has really been since the Europeans came to this continent and changed things so much, we are only at the chronological beginning of this trauma. There is still time to work against the disconnect, to reconcile with both land and people. I think that's why they invited you. Inviting you to the Sweat Lodge was a gesture of generosity. They are asking for your service, not just to report on them or be a passive witness."

"That's the part I wonder about. What can I *do*, in the end?"

"Well, what started you on all this in the first place?" Layli asked, changing the subject. "So you were looking for information on your hometown, you found out about the dam's impact, but then why get so fixated?"

"It was the rash of suicides," I replied. "I couldn't believe it when I read it. It happened last year—seven suicides in one month and then twenty-five more attempted suicides. At a school with five hundred or so students. Can you imagine? The council called a state of emergency, the Elders performed some ceremony—."

Layli cut me off. "Wait, what?"

"In the spring," I said. "Last March. The Elders, they declared a state of emergency and performed this ceremony calling the spirits of the land and the water and the sky to come help the young people in the community."

"Oh Kazim," she said, her voice dropping, and I couldn't tell if she was kidding or not, "they *called you*."

*

27

From Boston I will fly to Minneapolis and then on to Winnipeg, where I will catch a twelve-seater propeller plane that will carry me into the boreal forests of northern Manitoba.

In my pocket I have a plane ticket, my passport, and the origami crane. As I hand my ticket to the agent, I reach with my other hand into my pocket and hold the crane between my thumb and forefinger. The artist was following an old tradition of folding a thousand cranes to promote peace. I took one as a talisman for my journey back into a history I am worried about, not worried because it holds any danger for me, but worried because of everything that has happened in the forty years since. I imagine the crane's energy accompanying me on the journey, once more crossing a border, this time into my past.

How on earth am I going to experience that place?

I am not really even sure how I will spend the week. I know that I want to go back to the site of the old town of Jenpeg, the town made of trailers, but I don't even know where the site is or if it is there anymore. Beyond that, I'm not sure.

In Minneapolis, I think about presenting myself when they call for "global services" to board the plane. I feel like a diplomat, an ambassador for my family back to the people who were affected by the work we were a part of. Could it be true what Layli said yesterday, that the call of grief and shock radiated outward when the Pimicikamak council issued their state of emergency after the suicides? That suddenly this urgency entered the psychic stream and I began again to dream and think about the land of my childhood? Yes, only a month before when I emailed the Chief, I was freezing in the polar vortex, remembering the forests of my early childhood, trees I had not thought about in years or even decades.

That was the place I came into language, where I learned to read and to write, where I learned the names of countries and looked up into the night sky and learned about the stars and planets, and by learning the names of constellations I learned the myths of the Greeks. I first saw snow there, first knew death—before any other death, the death of a boy a few years older than me in school, a boy named Gus Letain, who died early in our time there.

And there was where I first learned about water: surrounded by it on every side, the lake, the snow, the ice, the sky—water cast its spell on me in its many forms.

One winter at school we were all given little squares of blue felt. We pulled on our snow boots, our parkas, our hats and mittens and trooped out to the schoolyard in the snow. We were supposed to hold up our squares of felt into the bright white afternoon sky and catch snowflakes. And there on the thick weave of felt we could observe their crystalline structure, provided we did not breathe directly on them and make them melt instantaneously away.

Of course my delight was in breathing hotly on them and watching them disappear, back into air.

The orange paper folded into a crane in my pocket is as delicate and small as the snowflakes we caught on the felt scraps. Like a grain, a small stone, a talisman.

3.

IN WINNIPEG, I take a cab from the international airport through the residential neighborhood that surrounds it, with uniform brick row houses and postage-stamp front yards, to the private airport of Perimeter Aviation, a regional company that uses an old runway of the main airport to service daily flights to the First Nations communities in northern Manitoba, including Cross Lake.

The terminal has the dimensions of a bus station in a small town. The runway is no bigger than a high school athletic field. It doesn't have to be very big for the twelve-seat propeller planes that fly out of here to Cross Lake, Norway House, Nelson House, Split Lake, and York Factory, the main northern communities.

For the first time I feel like I am in a space other than normative "Canadian" space. The art on the walls here, by Indigenous artists, depicts the trees and lakes I remember so well, and also the mountains of the west. The colors are green and brown, and the animals and people depicted in the paintings all call to mind the landscapes of the north. Nearly everyone waiting is an Indigenous person, and they are speaking to each other in their own language. No one is speaking English except when they go up to the ticket counter. I realize that the airline, which is not an Indigenous-owned business, is consciously trying to create an Indigenous-themed atmosphere here in the middle of Winnipeg, a border zone between this place called "Canada" and the communities they will fly us to.

Everyone is very relaxed. I notice that some of the older people in the crowd are dealing with various health issues. Many are using walkers or wheelchairs. Everyone is laughing and joking, raising their voices. The houses I grew up in were also loud with laughter and conversation. Nobody spoke quietly; you had to shout to be heard over everyone in the room. There in the terminal I had this weird sudden rush of feeling not alien any more—or at least not *as* alien.

Two women are duct taping their suitcases closed and there's an old man shuffling into the gate area carrying a tote bag bulging with snacks: chips, and cereal, and cheese puffs.

On the wall there is a map of Winnipeg and I find Bishop Grandin Boulevard. It was near that major artery that the houses of my family clustered. Before we moved north to Jenpeg, my father and mother had a small house at 317 River Road in the St. Vital neighborhood of Winnipeg, and my mother's eldest sister—who was married to my father's eldest brother—lived down the road close to the park at number 106. At first my grandparents and my mother's younger brother Safdar lived in rooms that my handy father constructed in our basement, but later on my grandparents and Safdar moved into the house at 23 Harmony Cove, just behind Bishop Grandin Boulevard. In addition to my grandparents and uncle Safdar, my other uncle Ifteqar also lived in that house before moving north to Thompson. Another uncle, Turab, moved into a house nearby, on St. Ann's Place, and a year later my mother's middle sister Jaffery and my father's middle brother Dilawer—who, yes, were married to each other—moved into a house around the corner at 163 Sterling Avenue. Another of my mother's sisters, Nadira, lived just half an hour away with her husband, an agricultural scientist. It was Jaffery's kitchen on Sterling Avenue that became the center of our family life. No matter

31

where we slept, it was Ammijaan—"dear mother," as we all called that particular aunt—who dished up our morning Weetabix into little wooden bowls, and prepared our lunchtime pickle sandwiches, and always had a plum or nectarine available for an afternoon snack. It was around her table each evening that epic *Clue* games took place, as all my uncles and aunts, with only a couple of cards apiece in their hands, tried to figure out whether it was Mrs. Peacock or Colonel Mustard who did the deed, while we kids stood around the edges, peeking, trying not to spill the beans.

As in any migrant family, everyone was doing what they could to make do. Safdar, who had a degree in accounting, was delivering circulars from the back of his big blue van. My uncle Dilawer—whom all of the cousins called "Baba" or "father"—worked as a night security guard, while Ammijaan cooked in a restaurant. Bolstered by her customers' enthusiastic response to her cooking, she began preparing her famed nimbu achar in bulk and bottling it to sell at the local Safeway. The grocery store manager, perhaps wanting to market the spicy lime pickle to as wide a Canadian market as possible, changed the brand name, printing bright green stickers that read "Jeffrey's."

I smile, thinking about all the family gatherings, the Saturday morning cartoon marathons, the bike rides, and the mornings we helped our uncle Safdar deliver the circulars; he'd pay us a penny for each one we carried from the van and stuffed into a mailbox. We called him "Chand-mamu," meaning "moon uncle," which over the years shortened to "Chanzy." Through all those early years, Chanzy never stopped the hustle. After the circulars he worked for a cleaning service, vacuuming strangers' homes. Then he started selling Amway and doing taxes. Yet no matter how hard he was working, there always seemed to be enough time to corral together a van-full of cousins for a quick drive down the street to Swede's for a round of slushies. A couple of years later after Safdar and my younger uncle Ifteqar returned to Pakistan briefly to get married—in a double wedding, naturally— their wives also moved into 23 Harmony Cove, and a year later each couple had a newborn.

I trace Bishop Grandin Boulevard on the map with my finger. That was also the road my grandfather Sajjad Sayeed died on. In July of 1980, after we had moved away, first to Staten Island, and then to Buffalo, while crossing the street on one of his constitutional walks, he was struck by a vehicle. How unfair—he wandered across the world, then came here to this strange city for just a few brief years. Walking in the summer, rambling through the neighborhood like he used to—what a strong no-nonsense man he was, but tender and even-keeled. Who was the driver that struck him? Where is that man now, and what happened to him? As far as I remember no one in my family has ever talked about this. Maybe we don't know. Our history is scattered across continents.

As for the man for whom the street was named, Vital-Justin Grandin was one the French bishops who supported religious conversions among the Indigenous Peoples and one of the earliest supporters of the residential school system. He believed it was vital to make sure that Indigenous children "forget the customs, habits, and language of their ancestors."

I wonder whether my father and the other engineers, or any of the white people who lived and worked in Jenpeg, ever wondered about what happened in the forty years that have followed since the dam's construction. Did anyone before me go back? And if they went back, did they go to the Jenpeg town site only? Did they get as far as Cross Lake?

In the airport-terminal bathroom there is a bin for biomedical waste, filled about six inches deep with discarded needles,

I am assuming for insulin. Besides the historical health challenges posed to Indigenous communities by disease and substance abuse, I've learned that because of the relatively recent and rapid changes in the traditional diets of Indigenous Peoples, nearly thirty percent of adults in Cross Lake suffer from diabetes, compared with less than five percent of the general population of Manitoba; children as young as seven years old are being diagnosed with type 2 diabetes, the adult onset variety of the disease.

It's eerie being back in Winnipeg. I haven't thought of the place in so long, but I realize that for me the air is still thick with memories of my family. My younger sister was born here; my grandfather died here and is buried here, and my uncle Turab is buried here too. He was a mechanic who also lived and worked in Jenpeg for a while, during our time there and for a year or two after. Is this how people who live in the same place their whole lives feel all the time, that the earth and air around you holds your history?

We are waiting to board in the small gate area past the single security checkpoint. There are twelve of us going to Cross Lake, five white people, five Indigenous people, a young man of East Asian descent, and me. They have not yet called us to board.

No one has been able to tell me whether there are roads now from Cross Lake to the old site of Jenpeg. I know in the old days, when we lived there, there weren't—and that at this time of year the lake will not be frozen. Would I even be able to get back there?

Before we pull out, the co-pilot hands out foam earplugs for us to wedge into our ears. Unusually, my auricles lack intertragic notches, so my ears cannot hold earplugs, but I push them in as far as I can and hold them in place with my fingers.

The plane lifts up over green forests toward Lake Winnipeg, which stretches from here all the way to Norway House and Cross Lake.

Looking down over the landscape as we fly north, it is no wonder my childhood memories are so filled with water. It's everywhere you look, the silver threads of the Red River and the Assiniboine River meeting and swirling into a tarnished gleam. And then north of the city the great blue dark of Lake Winnipeg fills our vision.

Rain begins to fall. We climb higher.

The plane shudders and it feels as if we are entering the water. I reach into my jacket pocket and brush the wing of the crane.

What is the origami artist's name, the woman who folded it? Suddenly I want to know. I would like to tell her—explain to her that I am being borne back to my originating place, my real hometown, where I came to English, borne there by her delicate bird.

4.

THE RAIN COMES down in solid sheets, drumming across the metal body of the airplane, water returning from the sky to the earth. It is a system that must travel freely, from air to ground to river, through a cycle. I think of Toni Morrison's words, "All water has a perfect memory and is forever trying to get back to where it was." I cannot help but think of myself, drawn back to a place that for years I had not thought of.

By the time the rain clears up we are in the north, passing the northern edge of Lake Winnipeg and flying over the traditional lands of Pimicikamak. Looking down at the green and blue landscape it is easy to see why it's named "Where a lake lies across the river." There are huge expanses of lakes interspersed with the land; there's nearly more water than earth down there, and countless rivers lace through. It's impossible to discern whether the patches of land are islands or peninsulas or whether the water one sees is a narrow lake or very wide river.

The water, so intrinsically part of the land here, surrounds the town that now materializes below us as we descend to the earth. Several rivers—including the Nelson—weave through the numerous lakes that surround the town of Cross Lake.

The terminal is no larger than my living room. The walls are a bright brown wood, and there are various maps of the region and safety notices taped up. There's a small ticket counter and eight or ten plastic chairs filled with people waiting for the flight back to Winnipeg. In the center of the room is another small row of chairs, occupied by an older woman with short-clipped hair speaking animatedly to a younger woman

36

who is wearing a Winnipeg Jets sweatshirt and taking notes in a notepad. As she's speaking, the older woman's eyes drift over to me and she gives me a wink and then pats the other woman's denim knee and rises up out of her chair to greet me. She is wearing a green winter jacket buttoned up to her throat. She smiles and her eyes sparkle as she opens her arms. I instinctively respond, and before any words are spoken between us, we embrace. In my ear she says, "You must be Kazim! I am so glad you have come!"

And that is how I meet Chief Cathy Merrick for the first time. As we pull back, she holds on to my elbow, keeping me in her embrace and introducing the woman beside her, who has also stood up. "This is my assistant, Sonia. I am going to Winnipeg for meetings but I will be back in a few days. Sonia is going to drive you to Lee Roy's house and he will make sure you are taken care of until I get back."

"Why are you going to Winnipeg?" I want to know.

"I have to get some money from the province," she declares, then hoists her carry-on bag and waves as she makes her way out to the tarmac with the other passengers.

"Nice to meet you," I say to Sonia, who does not respond. She turns and exits the terminal and so I follow.

"She moves fast," I say, catching up to Sonia. She turns and flashes me a big smile and laughs.

"Yes, she does!" She gestures toward a black pickup truck, its sides streaked with mud and dust. "This is the Chief's car."

I throw my suitcase in the truck bed and climb up into the passenger seat as Sonia takes the wheel. She flips a cassette of country music into the tape deck and pulls out of the muddy parking lot. The truck jounces as it rolls over the thick ridges in the dirt that years of tires have made and packed.

"Is Chief Merrick the first woman Chief in Cross Lake?"

"She actually isn't," Sonia says. "There was one other, many years ago, back in the 1970s while they were negotiating the Flood Agreement. An old woman who lived off the land up on the trap-line."

"Trap-line?"

"There's designated areas where every Band is allowed to trap, so we don't get in each others' ways. They have to be out farther from the community so everyone knows whose traps are where. Some people choose to live out there instead of in town."

We drive down the dirt road from the airport and one arm of the lake stretches out to our left. As I gaze out over the murky silver expanse this all feels very familiar—the glassy water, the dark fringe of high firs on the opposite side.

"Did you grow up in Cross Lake?" I ask.

"I did," Sonia says. "But I moved away to Brandon, in the southern part of the province, for college."

Sonia and I are close in age: she tells me that her oldest son is thirty; her daughter and her younger son are both still in school.

As we drive along the low causeway nearly even with the water, I see these big signs at the edge of town—small billboards really—with the faces of young people on them, labeled MISSING or MURDERED, with dates below and details about the cases. These remind me of the posters of Palestinian youth I have seen in the occupied territories, youth killed by the occupation forces. I wonder who these missing young men and women are, and whether the signs have been successful in solving the cases.

"I'm curious to know what brought you back," I say to Sonia, as we pass the MISSING and MURDERED signs and enter the outskirts of the town of Cross Lake.

"I guess it wasn't until I started to have kids that I felt like I wanted to come back here. I wanted my kids to grow up the same way I did, you know, going out on the lake in the summer, going hunting and fishing. I didn't want to raise them in the city."

Sonia's desire for her kids to have a connection to her home is made more poignant considering Canada's history of disrupting Indigenous family life by taking—against the wishes of their parents—Indigenous children and babies, often newborn, from their families and placing them with primarily white Canadian families to foster or adopt. Probably the most well-known of these efforts was the so-called Sixties Scoop. Tens of thousands of Indigenous children across the county were removed from their families, frequently with little pretext. Despite its nickname, the practice of family separation began much earlier and continued well into the 1980s. As with the residential school system, the family separations were devastating to the individual and to the community both, and in many cases resulted in loss of Status, by which Indigenous people receive benefits due them under the Indian Act, for First Nations children.

And yet, influential Canadian pundit and journalist Gary Mason and others have argued in national newspapers that a solution to the suicide epidemic in places like Cross Lake would be urban resettlement of the young population. The truth is that there are already many urban Indigenous communities. Those Indigenous Peoples who have migrated to the cities, mostly to the south, whether in search of housing or economic opportunities, or because they were forcibly taken from their communities by Canadian Family Services, have faced more difficulties than pundits like Mason have acknowledged, including housing and job discrimination and other kinds of structural racism. There has also been a documented pattern of sustained and historic abuses against Indigenous

Peoples by law enforcement, including the infamous "starlight tours," conducted by the Saskatoon Police Department in which Indigenous men who had been arrested were driven to the perimeter of the city in the dead of the winter, had their shoes taken from them, and then were abandoned, being told to walk home. Several men died of exposure from the late 1970s through the early 2000s. One man, Darrell Night, survived; his testimony brought charges. The two officers involved were convicted of unlawful confinement and sentenced to eight months in prison. Many of the disappearances of Indigenous Peoples, particularly of Indigenous women, remain unsolved, and even when arrests are made, murderers are acquitted.

In response to these grave challenges, some southern Indigenous urban communities have been organizing and building their own community organizations and institutions, such as Neechi Commons in Winnipeg. But the notion that compounding the original land theft of colonizers with a further forced relocation to urban centers would mitigate the challenges faced by Indigenous communities seems misguided at best and criminal at worst.

In general, Cross Lake is worn around the edges: it reminds me of the older neighborhoods in Albany, or of the towns in the West Bank territory in Palestine—the cold long winter here also weathers buildings faster. Things are old and don't get repaired, or they get jury-rigged back together. The buildings in Cross Lake are like those I remember in Jenpeg, corrugated steel, and many of them look pre-fabricated and temporary. But Cross Lake is far more spread out than Jenpeg was—here the streets are strung along the wide arms of the lake whose inlets separate the neighborhoods from one another. The center of town occupies a small strip where the parts of the lake converge. There are around six thousand people living in Pimicikamak Cree Nation reserve land, and about five hundred more people live on the surrounding provincial land and out on the trap-line. Nearly twenty-five hundred more Pimicikamak People live "off reserve," many of these in urban centers like Thompson, Brandon, and Winnipeg. I learn that much of the off-reserve migration is due to an extreme shortage of local housing. Only twelve units had been built in the past year, and to me the older buildings seem barely habitable, at least as viewed from the outside.

"Some of those houses look pretty rough," I remark to Sonia.

"Yeah," she says. "Lots of families have to live together because there aren't enough spaces."

"I know a little bit about that—I grew up with my extended family. It was my mom and dad, my sisters, my grandparents, and my uncle in our house in Winnipeg for a couple of years."

"Oh yeah?" she says. "It's even more people here, sometimes fifteen or more people living in one of those houses."

The house she points to, a green dwelling with crumbling concrete foundation, looks like an ordinary single-family home to me, and on the small side. The new houses under construction are also for single families, another example of how housing policies do not keep up with material conditions on the ground, nor with the cultural practices of communities the authorities are intending to serve.

We drive through the cold afternoon past the town and along one of the inlets toward Lee Roy's house. There are three children running and playing in a small, scrubby yard in front of one dilapidated green prefabricated house, similar to the ones I remember from Jenpeg. The side of the house, visible from the road as we drive past, is lettered in graffiti.

5.

WE DRIVE OUT of town heading north, the lake on our left. As the houses get farther and farther apart, Sonia slows down.

"Here's Lee Roy's place," she announces, and we pull into a dirt driveway that runs alongside and then behind the house, leading to a big shed in the backyard and an open area scattered with piles of branches and stones of differing sizes—from boulders it would take two people to lift to loose stones and gravel. Lee Roy, a tall, powerfully built man with long, coal-black hair pulled back into a neat ponytail, is outside, supervising two younger men as they heft larger boulders into a big fire that a third youth, a boy really, is continuously stoking.

"Hello, Kazim," he says, briskly shaking my hand. "Let me show you inside where we are going to do the Sweat."

Sonia and I shake hands goodbye, and I go into the big shed with Lee Roy. The physical sweat lodge itself takes up about three quarters of the space inside the shed. The lodge is built of willow wood and has blankets thrown over the wood frame to keep the heat in. It is situated on a plywood floor with a concrete fire pit in the middle for the heated stones. The stones are heated outside for a long time; the men will bring them in when we are ready to sweat.

The stones glow red from inside: they seem like they are alive, sparkling with embers. Big flat shovels are used to port the stones to a wooden trench that is positioned to slide the stones into the sweat lodge and down into the pit at its center. Each year at the end of the season, Lee Roy tells me, the lodge frame is given back to the earth and will be rebuilt with new branches and stones the following year.

"Kazim, we're going to keep working on the stones," says Lee Roy, "but let me introduce you to Mervin Dreaver." Lee Roy takes me to the other side of the shed where an elderly Cree man sits in a lawn chair, jaunty in a plaid, snap-button cowboy shirt and denim jeans. He's wiry thin and smoking a cigarette while balancing a styrofoam cup of milky tea on his knee. "Mervin, this is Kazim, he's come all the way from Ohio to sweat with us."

"Do you want some tea to warm up?" Mervin asks, gesturing behind him to where an electric samovar bubbles, and I nod. As Lee Roy excuses himself, I introduce myself to the other men who are sitting at Mervin's feet, two white men. Mike, a middle-aged Canadian man with an easy smile, is the provincial auditor assigned to the Cross Lake Band. He comes to Cross Lake often, and on this trip he has brought his friend Sean, a slim man of indeterminate age with a shock of brown curly hair, who I later learn is a reporter for the CBC, one of the main news outlets in Canada.

While Mervin turns around to pour out a cup of tea for me, Mike leans forward and says in a lowered voice, "Mervin's kind of a legend around here. He's a longtime activist and has some notoriety among the young people because a while back, in the '80s, when on a trip to Ottawa, he supposedly went into the Parliament building and confronted the prime minister."

"Really?" I say.

"Oh, it gets better. Ask him." Mike sits back as Mervin turns back to us and hands me a cup of tea.

"Mr. Dreaver," I begin.

"Oh no," he says, waving his hand around, "you have to call me Mervin." He lights another cigarette.

"Mervin, are you from Cross Lake?"

"I come out from Saskatchewan. I travel all through the northern Cree territories so I can teach the younger people about the old traditions."

"Like the Sweat?"

"Oh, how to do the Sweat, what the herbs are that, you have to gather, this knowledge is almost lost, only the older people hold it and we have to pass it along. This is the way for all the old laws and traditions. You have to know the prayers and the rituals, how we used to do it. How we pour the medicinal water onto the stones; how long you stay inside; how many times to do it—we don't write it anywhere, this is all passed down, you have to learn it from a teacher."

"Is it safe? Does the Canadian government regulate the Sweat Lodge rituals in any way? I mean, is there any certification process for who is or isn't allowed to claim the right of being able to facilitate the ceremony?"

"Hey!" he exclaims sharply, stabbing the air with his cigarette. "You're not in Canada right now," Mervin says. "This is Pimicikamak." He pauses. "We are the ones who pass this knowledge on to each other. No one has the right to claim this knowledge for themselves, nor to sell it or profit from it. You are on Treaty land. We follow Aboriginal laws here. These ceremonies are thousands of years old and only those who have been properly initiated into them are able to offer and supervise them." He softens a little and then reassures me, "You are safe here."

I do trust him, and legally speaking, of course, he's right. The land the dam was built on, and the waterway it controls— though claimed by Canada as within its physical and political territory—was never ceded by the people who live here: not by war, not by Treaty. In the late 1960s Prime Minister Pierre Trudeau's government sought to dismantle the 1867

Indian Act. Then Minister of Indian Affairs and Northern Development (note the not-unintentional dual purview of the portfolio) Jean Chrétien consulted Indigenous communities across Canada who wanted the Act amended but not abolished. They were not prepared to accept full suffrage in Canada at the expense of relinquishing their Indigenous identities and political and territorial sovereignty claims. Chrétien ignored the proposals and feedback from the Indigenous communities and instead presented the now infamous White Paper of 1969. The White Paper proposed to eliminate the Indian Act—thereby eliminating legal Indian status—and abolish the federal Department of Indian Affairs. They would then transfer all financial obligations to currently held Indigenous land, which would become private property, to the provinces. The existing Treaties would be phased out, and Indigenous Peoples would become full citizens of Canada without any remaining rights as Indigenous Peoples. Needless to say, Indigenous activists were furious, and the Indian Chiefs of Alberta issued a manifesto dubbed the "Red Paper," calling for, among other things, the existing treaties to be honored and the granting of full Indigenous sovereignty on lands currently held in trust by the Crown. Not until 1995 did Canada recognize Indigenous rights to self-government, though it stopped short of acknowledging the political sovereignty of Indigenous communities as Nations themselves. Subsequent court decisions have reaffirmed aspects of Indigenous sovereignty, including hunting and fishing rights; meanwhile, in legal terms the land and water where the dam is located has only been leased from the Cross Lake Band and is still covered by the agreement made with the band by Manitoba Hydro along with the provincial and federal governments. And, although in 2017 the federal government under Prime Minister Justin Trudeau vowed to create a Nation-to-Nation relationship to recognize the rights of Indigenous Peoples, it also continues to support the gas and oil industry, as well as expand hydroelectric development, despite deep resistance from Indigenous communities across Canada. The arrests of Wet'suwet'en activists in British Columbia—moves fully supported by the Trudeau government—in order to facilitate the construction of a pipeline through Wet'suwet'en lands is but one recent example.

Mervin goes on, "The landless government in Ottawa pretends that they own this land, but we are not on Crown land here, we are on Treaty land. We never ceded this land. And they have never stopped wanting it."

Several other young Pimicikamak men have come in while he was talking and they start nodding.

"Canada for as long as it has existed has been waging a continuous war on the identity, culture, and language of all the Cree in the north," Mervin says. "To this day. That is why I have to come out here and teach these young people!"

He acknowledges the new arrivals and each of them comes over to him and crouches down next to his chair to embrace him. He pats them each on the head gently and gives each one a quiet blessing.

"How often do you come?" I ask.

"Oh, I come out to Pimicikamak once a month maybe. I have to fly down from my reserve to Regina, and then on to Winnipeg, and then I fly up here. It's not an easy journey. In the old days you know, in the older days, you could get in a boat and come across the waterways. Those rivers fed our land but they were our highway too. The Saskatchewan River comes all the way from the BC border into the lake, and then the old folks could go on to the Bay or else portage to Cross Lake and get anywhere in Ontario or Quebec. We had a water highway!" Mervin laughs.

These rivers are dammed now—seven different dams obstructing, diverting, and harnessing the power of the rivers in northern Manitoba and Saskatchewan, so one can no longer travel directly from Big River First Nation, where Mervin lives, to Cross Lake.

"Mervin, I heard you used to go to Ottawa," I say then.

"Oh, you heard that, did you?" says Mervin chuckling. "Well, I can't go there anymore. I better not."

"Did you really confront Prime Minister Mulroney?" I ask.

"What do I care what he calls himself? He's not *our* prime minister. He needed to hear from us. Who was going to tell him about what is happening up here in the north when he is so far way over there?"

"But why can't you go back?" I ask, and Mike flashes me a little smile, nodding.

"Oh well, after I talked to Mulroney, after they hurried him off somewhere, I hung back. I snuck into the library of the Parliament building; I brought my pipe with me. I smoked sacred tobacco in there. My smoke is still hanging in the air there—they can't get away from me!"

I cover my mouth not in shock but to cover my smile. I don't think he's pulling my leg.

"Look, there is a reason we are standing up and resisting still, even after all this time and all these years. It is not just our own communities we are trying to protect, it is the whole of the planet. All the diseases that have come, all the storms raging, all the earthquakes. The earth itself is shifting in response to the actions of humans. In response to what we are doing. These are serious times." He speaks earnestly and rests his hand on my knee as he speaks. He looks right into my face and I have to force myself not to look away from the intensity, the entreaty, in his focused gaze.

47

And as for what he is saying, it doesn't feel that far-fetched to me.

Lee Roy comes back in and asks me if I brought anything as an offering. I haven't.

He suggests that since they will be heating stones for a while yet, one of the young men, Conley, could take me to the store to pick up an offering.

"What is a traditional offering?" I ask him.

"Any gift," he says. "Tobacco is traditional."

I notice that most of the men are smoking a brand called Canadian Classics. Conley and I set out in his pickup truck. He is young, as young as some of my students. He is very energetic and has a bright smile. As soon as we get in the truck, he starts asking me about all the places I've lived. When I mention my years in New York City, he gets excited. He wants to go on vacation there.

"Why there specifically?" I ask him.

"Oh, it's because they have all different kinds of food. I want to go to every restaurant there is and eat food from all around the world!"

I ask him what food he most wants to try, and he says without hesitation, "Sushi."

"Is it true you grew up in Jenpeg?" he asks then. We start talking about our families. He tells me that he has a four-year-old son, and then asks if I have children. I laugh a little and say no. He is silent for a moment, his eyes on the road, and then he says, "You must be a Two-Spirited guy then, right?"

"I am," I say.

"For us Cree," he says, "the Two-Spirited are respected because they are not empty, they are full—they have both the masculine and feminine in them."

"So everyone here is comfortable with Two-Spirited people?" I ask him.

He laughs. "Well, the people who follow traditional beliefs definitely are," he says. "The Christians though, they have ideas of their own."

While we are waiting in line at the store, two women in the line behind us ask me if I'm a teacher at the school. Conley tells me later that she probably thought that because outsiders are rare here in Cross Lake, though there are a few, including some teachers at the high school. I think of the other non-Indigenous people who were on the plane with me. I wonder what they do in Cross Lake.

We drive back to Lee Roy's place, and I put the packs of cigarettes I've bought on the small altar with the other offerings.

"Before you go in," says Lee Roy, "you should take Mervin's blessing, too."

I walk over to where Mervin still sits in the lawn chair. I kneel down in front of him as I had seen the other young men do. I lean toward him and he places one hand gingerly on top of my head. In a soft voice I say, "I am not sure what I am doing here."

I know he knows that I don't just mean the act of taking his blessing, nor the Sweat Lodge either. He leans forward to whisper in my ear, "You will find out. We're going to clear your head and the land will show you. Pimicikamak will show you."

There are ten of us—Mervin, Lee Roy, Conley, Mike, Sean, me, and several other young men who have joined us—who strip down to our shorts and climb into the lodge. The two men who were shoveling stones and the young boy with them remain outside. We sit, pressed shoulder to shoulder, in a small circle inside the sweat lodge.

The stones in the center gleam red-gold. I had thought of bringing the paper crane inside to be immolated against the stones in the sweat lodge, but I'd left it in the pocket of my jacket, hanging off the back of Mervin's chair; I had decided I want to have it with me throughout my time here.

In the darkness Mervin and the others begin chanting in their throats. It sounds to me so much like Urdu but probably this is because that's the language in which I last heard chants of such spiritual purpose—the mourning *marsiyya* the Shi'a Muslims sing in the month of Muharram.

There are four rounds of Sweat. After each round, men are able to exit the lodge and rest, or you can stay. I stay. I want to sweat everything out. The two men who remain outside the lodge, whose job is to bring the stones and keep the blanket covers closed, are also available in case anyone has physical distress. We all have water bottles inside to drink from.

During the Sweats, Mervin throws herbs and water onto the stones and they rush and hiss into steam, and we all breathe deeply. The herbs are pungent and penetrate one's nostrils and sinuses and skin. It gets so hot inside that I *feel* the steam entering into me, carrying with it the medicine and borne on Mervin's words. Suddenly dizzy, my childhood wells up inside me, images flashing through my mind, images of my childhood in Jenpeg—friends from school, the feeling of the toboggan's edge on my knees, the rope in my hands as I lean back to increase our speed on the slippery snow slope; three of us on one toboggan, screaming in glee. I hear the voice of my mother calling me in and then my teacher Miss Collins counting numbers and then the sounds of the gravel roads crunching under wheels of cars. I hear bird calls. For long moments I feel as if I am there, not here in the dark sweat lodge remembering but *there*, there in the Jenpeg that doesn't exist anymore.

And then Mervin lights a long pipe and passes it around the circle. In the black dark, the small orange light of the lit

50

pipe being smoked by each man in turn matches the central glow of the heated stones. Water in the air and on my skin, in my nose, in my mouth. We smoke the sacred tobacco together, one bowl, then two bowls, and then I hear Mervin saying through the haze, "Now you will really start to have dreams."

The men keep singing. The song drifts into minor keys, and in the dark I see the face of my mother's father, Sajjad Sayeed, calm, serene as I had always known him, his mouth turned down in a resting frown, his eyes clear and fixed on me. I had finally come back to this place in the north, where my father's father, my Ava, also lived for a little while—in dark, thick heat I feel goose bumps rise along my skin. Maybe I am not such a stranger here. Even though Sajjad Sayeed died a long way south from here, his spirit somehow rises into my consciousness adrift in the song that is being sung deep in the throats of Mervin and Lee Roy and the other men.

6.

WE ALL EMERGE from the sweat lodge slowly, tenderly, still a little dizzy but somehow refreshed.

"Drink water," says Lee Roy. "And don't bathe tonight. Let the herbs on your skin and in your hair stay there."

The boy—maybe twelve, named Lexis—has stayed behind to clean up after, to clear away the branches, sweep, put away the tea supplies. He notices the tattoos on my forearms, one in Sanskrit on my right arm and one in Farsi on my left arm.

"Hey, what do those mean?" he asks me, fixing me in his limpid, glass-green gaze.

"Well, this one is from an old yogic text: it says, 'Now is the time to study yoga,'" I explain. "This other one," I gesture to my left forearm, "is a line of poetry from Iran. It says 'I am a Muslim; the rose is my *qibla*.'"

"What's *qibla*?" he asks.

"*Qibla* means the direction to Mecca. When you are Muslim and you pray, you turn in the direction of a city in Saudi Arabia where a very ancient mosque is located."

"But that says the *rose* is the *qibla*. Which rose?"

"Any rose," I say. "Any rose in the world is the direction for my prayers. Not the place in Mecca, but a single rose."

"You're like us," the boy said seriously then, looking me in the eye. "You're plugged in."

But I don't *feel* plugged in. I feel a world away now. I am the one who feels lost and landless, a stranger out of time.

After the Sweat Lodge we go into Lee Roy's house. It is small and well kept, with nice hardwood floors and the wood-paneled walls I remember so well from my 1970s childhood. And, as in the houses of my childhood, no one wears shoes inside. The porch has cardboard spread all over the floor, and that is where everyone kicks off their shoes or boots, caked heavy with the ever-present mud and muck of the wintry ground outside.

In the dining room, there is a high table that takes almost the whole space. Lee Roy's wife, Loretta, was cooking while we were in the Sweat. She has made a neckbone stew and an un-leavened, pan-fried bread. I've been vegan for years, but before I embarked on my trip I realized that I would need to be flexible and omnivorous, not just because of what would be available but also to take part in peoples' hospitality. The bones have been long cooked so the meat and marrow inside are very tender.

I slather margarine on the bread and sop up broth. This bread, commonly called "bannock" after the Scottish bread it resembles, was a staple throughout the North American conti-nent for countless generations, typically made of maize or acorn flour, or from the bulbs of the camas plant, indigenous to North America.

I want to ask Mervin to explain the origins of the Sweat Lodge, but I am not sure how to ask. I feel conscious of being an outsider, and the ceremonies of the Sweat are ancient and may be proprietary knowledge.

As we sit and eat, Mervin, without any prompting, begins to tell us a little more about the Sweat Lodge traditions. "There are one hundred and four spices that go into the medicine," he says. "It's not written down anywhere, but we learned it from the ones who came before."

Remembering that there had been ten men in the lodge, I ask, "Do women ever participate in the Sweat?"

Lee Roy says, "Traditionally they don't. We are taught that they already have so much spiritual power that it could be potentially dangerous for them. Also some people say that because of their powerful natures they may draw all the beneficent energy toward them, and others present would not be able to receive any."

"Is it women who gathered the spices or do the men do that also?"

Mervin says, "In fact, traditionally it was the 'Two-Spirited' men who did this work."

Confirming what Conley had said to me earlier, Lee Roy says, "Two-Spirited men are considered sacred in Cree culture."

But what about Two-Spirited people—men and women both—who want to live in so-called heteronormative family structures?

"Are there Two-Spirited people in Cross Lake today?" I ask.

"Of course," Lee Roy answers, appearing to be puzzled at my question.

I think to myself that I would like to meet them, but again I don't really know how to ask. It feels awkward. I start keeping a mental list of the things I want to do and the people I want to meet when I next return. That's when it occurs to me that I already want to return here, a place I'd never been before and where until now I'd known no one.

Maybe it's because the town of Jenpeg is gone, the trailers pulled up and hauled away, the people having moved on, or back to wherever it was they came from. It's true that I have always thought that I have no hometown, but being here again among these tall trees, below this washed-out blue sky, triggers something deep and lonely inside me, something close to a homesickness.

"We're very blessed that Mervin comes to teach us," Lee Roy says. "There are so few people now versed in the old ways because of all the years of missionary work and the Indian schools. They always wanted us to stop. In fact, there are many Aboriginal People even now who distrust the traditional methods." He turns to me then. "You're going to meet a lot of people this week. Not everyone is so open to our traditional practices. Some are Christian, and they just look the other way when we do our Sweats, but other people, they reject the old ways completely."

I'm surprised and say so. Only a few weeks ago, Lee Roy tells me, a sweat lodge structure of one of his friends was vandalized and burned down, just down the road from the house where we're sitting.

"Lee Roy, you use the term 'Aboriginal,' but I had understood that the more commonly accepted term is 'Indigenous.'"

"Yeah," he rumbles. "That's what people are shifting to now. I say 'Aboriginal' because that is what we are. We have been here for longer than any history can remember, before there was writing, before anyone knows. Indigenous means we have some rights over the land, but it's beyond that. We're connected to the land, we're part of it, but it doesn't *belong* to anyone."

"So you wouldn't say Cree?"

"Well, everyone has a different name for us!" he says. The men around the table laugh. "Canada calls us the Cross Lake Band. We call ourselves Pimicikamak Cree Nation, but that's not accurate either. 'Cree' is a French word. We use it to talk about ourselves in English, but it's not the word we use in our own language. 'Cree' is what the French called all the people across northern Canada. It's not our word. And when you say "First Nations" or "Pimicikamak Nation" you are using a word from your own understanding of a relationship between a land and a people that has a political context different from our belief system. We don't view our traditional lands as a 'Nation' with borders and restrictions around who can be there or not be there."

"That is what got us into trouble in the first place," quips Mervin, and everyone laughs again.

"The land belongs to no one," asserts Lee Roy again. "It is its own. If anything, we belong to it. There is no 'nation' here, just the land and the people who live on it and with it. The trees, the stones, the water—they have rights to this place, they are *included* in it."

Being here on this land, in one of the many landscapes of my family, a place I remember my grandfather, a place my uncle Turab lived and died in, makes me think also of the presence of my father.

It's been a while since I have talked to him, and I wonder if having been here might help me to talk to him more and learn about what it was like for *him*, a young Pakistani man, to move his family across the globe, up into the northern reaches of a cold continent, to be so far from what was familiar to him. Or was he thinking about it at all? Would he, like my mother, be quizzical at my interest? I think about how I must return home and recount this trip to him.

And what if I truly was called by the ceremony of the Elders to come here? Aren't we all being called by waves and waves of what has been traditionally thought of as "past"? And yet, is the past "passed?" I smile, thinking of my old school booklet's page, labeled "September 35." Now some quantum theorists are saying that, in fact, it is very likely that particles are entangled both "forward" and "backward" through what we call "space-time," and the future can affect the past too. This seems to make sense to me, so often do I arrive at a point in my life that I am sure I have already lived.

As Mike and Sean prepare to leave, back to their motel, I go with them so I can book a room as well. The motel is a series of joined trailers in a dirt lot across from the hockey rink.

It's attached to a lightly stocked general store with a small grill. The motel is owned by three brothers, the Hillikers, who hail from Montreal and moved north to Cross Lake many years ago. My room is modern and comfortable, and I am exhausted from the day, still floating a little bit from the experience of the Sweat Lodge.

Lee Roy had told us not to shower right away, to let the herbs penetrate our skin all night, so I go to sleep with my hair still smelling of sweet smoke.

7.

LEE ROY HAD suggested I meet Jackson Osborne, a local Elder and historian. To drive me he sends Donald, a young man with a shaved head, round glasses, and a quiet air. We head back north along the lake in silence. We pass a small skate park and come to a driveway that serves three houses. Several dogs roam the yard. It seems like everyone has dogs here, and no one keeps them inside.

Jackson's house is small and modest, an actually constructed house unlike the pre-fabricated trailers we saw in town. When Donald knocks, Jackson does not answer.

"Maybe he's not home?" I ask.

"No, he's home," says Donald. I'm not sure how he knows; perhaps he knows Jackson's car, or perhaps there is nowhere for Jackson to go. Donald opens the door. It slides across a little square of cardboard that has been laid inside the house to collect the ubiquitous mud. Donald calls out Jackson's name across the small living room. Jackson comes around the corner from the kitchen area. He is a small man with inquisitive eyes blinking behind big glasses. He is wearing a blue housecoat and has a jar of instant coffee in one hand and a tablespoon in the other. It's obvious he is not expecting us.

Donald explains, "Jackson, this is Kazim. He grew up in Jenpeg when they were building the dam. He's come back to find out what is happening in Cross Lake."

Jackson's eyes light up and he nearly crows with excitement, "You grew up in Jenpeg! You've come back! You came back to see us!" He gestures us in. We remove our shoes on the cardboard and Jackson waves us toward the dining table while he bustles around the kitchen making coffee for us.

The kettle is barely on the stove when he exclaims, "I have so much to show you!" Before I can say anything in response, he is off, disappearing up a short flight of stairs from the living room, which must lead to the bedrooms. I hear him clapping his hands and talking to himself. Donald smiles a small smile. We hear much shuffling of papers and the sounds of drawers being opened and shut. Jackson reappears with two shoeboxes, which he places on the table between us, dragging his chair around so it's next to mine. He sits and opens the boxes. They are full of photographs.

"Look at these," he says. "These are photographs of Cross Lake. I go out in all different times of the year and take pictures of the lake shore so I can track the changes. See these shores?" He points to the shoreline in the photographs. He turns one photo over, and written there in spidery ballpoint is *Oct. 1989.* "Now I'll take you out to the same place and show you the photograph and show you the shore, and you can see for yourself what happened."

We sit and drink coffee while he pulls more photographs out of boxes to show to Donald and me. Jackson is something of a local historian, Lee Roy had told me.

"How many pictures do you have?" I ask him.

"Oh, these are only part of them. I've been taking pictures going back to the 1980s. I didn't start out taking pictures though. I started out trying to get the schools to teach Cree language. My whole family was in the residential school system, you know."

"I guess most of the older people in Cross Lake were," I said.

"That's right. And the whole time we were in there, we were serving Canada. My great-grandfather James Whiskey, he fought for Canada and was killed in the First World War.

And even though I have all these pictures here, we don't have any pictures of him and no medals, nothing to remember him by, just our stories."

He gets up to pour the coffee and brings the cups back to the table for the three of us. "I have never even been to his burial place. It's in Europe somewhere, with the other Canadian soldiers."

We're quiet for a moment, while we stir sugar into our cups.

"My aunt went to the residential school near Brandon and she didn't come back," he says then. "Her name was Betsy Osborne. She caught tuberculosis in the school and was sent to the sanatorium in Ninette, near Brandon, for medical testing. She died, but they never sent the body home. We don't even know where she is buried."

I am silent. Jackson looks out the window. Donald doesn't say anything either. As I learn later, this kind of occurrence was not uncommon. Often the children who died in the residential schools, whether from the medical testing, from the rigors of hard labor, or from suicide, were buried in unmarked graves.

"Well, then in 2011, there was a monument built," Jackson recounts, "and a ceremony held for those who were subjected to medical testing, but my sister's name wasn't on the list of names." He pauses. "So now we don't know *what* happened to her, when she died or where. Or how." In 2018, Anne Lindsay, a researcher in Brandon was able to locate the mass grave of 50 children from the residential school there, in what is now an RV park, by following a map that was hand-drawn for her by one of the residential school survivors. In contrast, there is still little information about the tuberculosis patients who were sent to the sanatorium. One former employee claimed in 2009 that there were upwards of two hundred former patients buried in underbrush a short drive from the facility.

Jackson's family, like mine, is connected to the dam: his father worked as a porter and guide for the original Manitoba Hydro team that surveyed the river in 1964. "Oh, he was always happy, always cracking jokes," says Jackson. "Here's some pictures of him with the team," he says, passing them over. In all the pictures I see of Charlie Osborne, he is smiling. In one of them, Charlie is wearing the camp cook's white hat and apron and is pretending to cook.

"Later," continues Jackson, "after the survey was complete and Hydro built the dam and the water levels started fluctuating, he regretted the work he did in helping the team to do the survey of the river. He is the one who told me to get a camera, to take pictures and document everything that was happening because of the dam."

To this day, Jackson goes out regularly at all times of the day and in all seasons of the year to take photographs of the same views of the shoreline, so he can collate them together and assemble evidence of the shore erosion. He began in 1988, he tells me, around ten years after the dam opened.

"Do you have any photographs?" he asks suddenly. "From before the dam was there? Do you think there are any early photographs in your parents' house?" he asks. "We don't have any here. All we have is the memory of the Elders."

"I don't think so, Jackson. But I will check," I promise. Even as I am saying this I am quite sure my parents don't have anything like that.

Suddenly Jackson reaches out and takes my hand and holds it in both of his and says earnestly, "Thank God you came. You are the first person who came back."

I'm a little surprised. "No one else from Jenpeg has come here in the past forty years?"

"From Hydro, sure. From the government, sure. Other people come too. Robert Kennedy Jr. came. Someone from the United Nations came once. But not the people. No one who lived there. Not out here to Cross Lake. People from Jenpeg used to drive over and buy our crafts, buy gloves and moccasins and mukluks. Then they left and went back to the cities. They never came back. You grew up here. You lived here. You're part of this land. This was your home, wasn't it? You're like us."

He stops and lifts his hands up toward the ceiling dramatically. "You've come back! Oh thank God for bringing you back!"

I smile at his passion even though I doubt I will be able to fulfill whatever hopes he is hanging on my presence.

"What would you do if others from Jenpeg came?" I want to know.

"I want to talk to them, the people who lived in Jenpeg and helped build the dam. They should know what happened," he says.

I promise that eventually I will share what I learn with everyone, with as many people as I can reach, anyhow. It occurs to me that not only the people who lived in Jenpeg but also any person who receives power from this dam ought to know what is happening.

We continue to look at his photographs. He shows me some big floating branches in the river. What happens, he explains, is that because of shore erosion, after the trunks rot and the soil breaks apart, the root systems of the dead trees float off into the river. They are called "spiders" and they interfere with the motors of boats and sometimes cause them to capsize.

The water rises and falls because of the dam, the shore is chewed away, and the trees die; in the pictures Jackson shows me it almost looks like a tornado has come through and shattered those trees.

"People get trapped," he says. "Sometimes they drown." He looks down at his hands. He says, more softly, "I wish your Dad could come here."

I say, "I bet he would like it here. When you talk to me you can imagine that you are talking to him. I will tell him what you say."

But I wonder how I will be able to explain all of this.

"It isn't only the Pimicikamak who have suffered," says Jackson then. "Even the animals who used to live with us don't come around Cross Lake anymore."

Changes in silt levels have made Cross Lake's water undrinkable, and sediment has affected the spawning patterns of local fish populations: now the sturgeon, the whitefish, and the pickerel are gone. And without the fish, the muskrats, the wolverines, the bears, and the beavers are gone, too; there's no more trapping and there's very little hunting. One has to drive far out past the old trap-lines to hunt for deer and moose, Jackson says. Some people commission small planes to fly them even farther, often several hundred kilometers into the forest to hunt.

There is another community a little upriver called Norway House, at the main channel of the Nelson River where it comes into Lake Winnipeg, where the sturgeons used to spawn. A team led by Annemieke Farenhorst in the Soil Sciences Department of the University of Manitoba came to study the drinking water here and changes in the lake's ecosystem due to construction of the Jenpeg Generating Station. One of the researchers, Johanna Theroux, was able to show that silt levels had, in fact, increased due to Manitoba Hydro's dredging of two natural channels from the Nelson River into Lake Winnipeg. The work was done in the early 1970s at first to try to manage flooding in the southern part of the province, though the potential for hydroelectrical development was quickly realized. Yet, the waters at Norway House seemed unaffected: most of the silt from the resulting erosion was being carried into the western channel, bypassing Norway House and more heavily impacting the waters around the community of Cross Lake.

How was this allowed to happen? The province began surveying the northern river systems in the mid-1960s; by 1971 it had determined, based on survey reports, that the Nelson was ideal for generating hydroelectricity and that its flow could be increased by diverting several other waterways into the Nelson both before and after the dam. Brian Grover, the leader of the original survey team, wrote that the waters of the Nelson were "clear, of high quality, so clean and fresh that we drank it directly from the river."

The province set about negotiating terms with the five First Nations that would be affected by the changes in water level. These included Cross Lake, Nelson House, Norway House, Split Lake, and York Factory, a community that had been previously relocated from their original site at the mouth of the Nelson River on Hudson Bay. Although construction began in 1974, it wasn't until 1977 that the five bands came to terms with Manitoba Hydro, the provincial government, and the federal government in the treaty called the Northern Flood Agreement.

"Do you have a copy of the actual treaty?" I ask Jackson.

"I do!" he exclaims, jumping up and hurrying up the small staircase and down the corridor again. He emerges again with a booklet of photocopied papers held together by an old-fashioned metal fastener like we used to use in school. We sit and peruse the treaty. It's a slender document, running about seventy-five pages and full of legal language that traffics in promises to remediate the environmental impact of the dam, even while it is careful to say such outcomes are unknown and unpredictable and full remediation may prove impossible. The bulk of its pages are devoted to legal processes, describing terms and defining arbitration and implementation structures. The pages that make actual agreements with the bands are few and sparse in details, even though at the very beginning of the document all parties agree unequivocally, "As a result of the Project, the water regime of certain waters, rivers, lakes and streams has been or will be modified." Somewhat more ominously, all parties also agree that it is "not possible to foresee all adverse results" of the dam's construction. Accepting an offer to compensate each participating band with a 4:1 ratio of acres in exchange for lands ceded, the Cross Lake Band surrendered all land on their reserve contiguous to the Nelson River and lower than 690 feet above sea level.

An essential part of the treaty was a promise by Manitoba Hydro that they would "control the flow of water on the regulated waterways so they do not exceed 687 feet above sea level" and that they would "prevent inundation of Reserve lands." Neither of these provisions has been effectively managed. It was in light of these abrogations, that in 2014 the Pimicikamak contested Manitoba Hydro's rights to those ceded lands by occupying the site of the Jenpeg Generating Station and serving eviction papers.

Other parts of the treaty deal with ensuring potability of water from the lake, preservation of archeological and cultural sites, management of wildlife resources, and funding for social, economic, and cultural development in Cross Lake.

Most people I meet in Cross Lake know generally about the terms of the treaty but not the specifics. Generations of mistrust at the intentions of the both provincial and federal authorities led the chiefs, including Walter Monias of Cross Lake, to hire their own attorneys as negotiators on their behalf. After fours years of intensive negotiations, at 4:00 am after an all-day and all-night session, Monias, the chair of the chiefs' committee, finally conceded that there was no choice but to sign the agreement. Like the men who negotiated Treaty 5, he perhaps saw that conceding to the dam's construction, and accepting the treaty's promises of economic development, might be the best chance for the future. Nonetheless, in a gesture of lingering, though symbolic resistance, he insisted that their negotiating team—white Canadians—sign the document first before any of the Indigenous chiefs would. In a way, by the carrying out of this small yet significant breach in protocol, the chiefs were expressing that they truly felt they had no choice. Even after all the negotiations, when the treaty was presented to the community for ratification, only 57% of the voters in Cross Lake voted to ratify, as opposed to much higher percentages in the other affected communities.

Jackson has suggested that there be a community workshop in which they all sit down and study the Agreement and learn about what is in there, so they can organize their future activism.

In the years after the construction of the dam, when the environmental impacts had become known and when the stated promises of the Northern Flood Agreement for support of economic and social development as well as environmental protections were abrogated, the original survey team leader Brian Grover came to regret his role in surveying the river and enabling construction of the dam. The extreme underdevelopment in Cross Lake, the community that had participated in the surveys and had hosted and assisted with the building of the dam, distressed him.

"First Nations people," he wrote in his 2016 memoir *The Summer of '64 on the Nelson River*, "who were present long before immigrant settlers arrived from many other countries, should be able to enjoy the high standard of living which most other Canadians have achieved." He recognized that the mineral and energy wealth of Indigenous Peoples has been diverted and does not provide them with material benefits. Grover, too, speaks of Charlie Osborne's regret with sadness: "Charlie reportedly told his family that he regretted having done the work he did—with me and with many other technical people from southern communities. He stated that he would not have done this work if he had understood the consequences which followed." His book is dedicated to the four members of his survey team from Cross Lake, including Charlie Osborne.

Grover's remembrances, like my own, were not incidental. His renewed interest and the writing of his memoir stemmed from the same sense of urgency that drew me back to Jenpeg and Cross Lake—the suicide epidemic among the young people that winter. Grover had realized that while the vast majority of material benefits from the dams in the north go to residents of the southern parts of the provinces—and also to some northern US cities in Minnesota and North Dakota—the environmental, economic, and social costs are borne by the northern Indigenous populations.

As Grover points out, because the difference in elevation between Lake Winnipeg and Hudson Bay is more than two hundred meters, the waterway that connects them is especially valuable as a source of hydroelectric power; besides the Jenpeg Generating Station, there are three other dams across the Nelson River on its way to Hudson Bay, and most of the smaller rivers and streams on the route have been diverted into the Nelson to increase its flow. These diversions along the waterways of the north have caused immense shore erosion, including here in Cross Lake. Contrary to the original intention of opening the channels, the disruption of normal water flow across the province has resulted in intermittent flooding for towns abutting the major lakes, even in the south, that disproportionately affect Indigenous communities.

Lake St. Martin is probably the most famous recent example; in 2011 there was a large and irregular spring runoff in the streams and rivers around the city of Winnipeg; to protect valuable properties there, the province diverted floodwaters onto reserve land. The community of Lake St. Martin was evacuated and subsequently destroyed by the floodwaters. For six years the lost town's nearly fifteen hundred residents lived in temporary housing in Winnipeg. Only in 2017 were some of the residents finally resettled back in Lake St. Martin; ninety-two elderly members of the community had died in the intervening years. As of early 2020, approximately 314 families were still waiting for housing to be built so they could return home. Those who had already returned were still lacking jobs, healthcare facilities, and social services.

Jackson recounted to me other ways the relationship with the lake has changed. Besides the so-called "spiders," which threaten the motorboats, some of the small islands where people used to live have been flooded and made uninhabitable, all their residents had to be evacuated to the mainland.

"The lake is an essential part of our identity here," says Jackson. "The water is as sacred to us as the land. It is a part of our lives as much as the earth and the sky. The water is the blood that sustains us. It must flow for our land to be healthy."

As Mervin had explained to me, Cree lands all across northern Canada were connected not only by the free-flowing water but by culture and language. While there were various Indigenous peoples who waged war over territory, resources and access to trade, throughout their history the Pimicikamak never had a military tradition, nor did they engage in territorial expansion or acquisition. Their way of life since time immemorial was sustainable, from the abundance of fishing, hunting, and trapping, supplemented by the relatively fertile agriculture of the water-fed region. So tied to their livelihood is their connection to water that it is reflected in the name the people of Pimicikamak once called themselves: *nikikonakos*—"otter people."

"We are not just trying to save the lake and the fish, but we are trying to save ourselves as a people," Jackson insists.

All along, there have been activists attempting to help the community. There is an activist couple named Tommy and Rita Monias, whose picture Jackson shows me, who have been working for decades on mitigation plans to reverse some of the flood-related damages. Some Hydro employees, including Ruth Christensen and Merv McKay, also tried to help, Jackson tells me. Even Len Bateman, the CEO of Hydro during the dam's construction, who was a proponent of hydroelectric energy as a cleaner form of energy than coal, knew that the environmental impacts of the dam were exceeding what had been expected. The name Monias is familiar, of course, as Walter Monias was the Chief who signed the Agreement, but I've seen it elsewhere too, though I can't remember where.

"I want to show you some more pictures," Jackson announces. "Come!"

We go back into the room where he has stored his archives. It's small, and seems to be still serving as someone's bedroom, probably a child. There's a single bed propped up on

69

top of two dressers on one side, and a desk and filing cabinets on the other side. He pulls another big box out from under the desk. "I have some videos in here, too."

On the corkboard above the desk there is a beautiful ink drawing of an abstract design, sort of like clouds. "Who did this?" I ask Jackson, touching the drawing.

"Oh, my nephew Charlton," Jackson says, brushing his fingers across the drawing. "He was an artist. I have a folder with his drawings." And he pulls out a folder bulging with scraps of paper and drawings—of people, of animals, wild abstractions.

"Where is he now?" I ask, afraid of the answer.

"He drowned on the lake," says Jackson. "His boat was capsized by a spider and they didn't get out there in time to save him."

I don't say anything.

"Come on," says Jackson, putting the folder back. "Let's take a drive."

8.

WE DRIVE OUT, Donald and Jackson and I, to see the places the water has flooded the lands, where the shore has eroded away.

On our drive, I am captivated anew by the quality of the northern light. It always looks like it's been raining: the yellow-white golden color of the dry grasses; the muted green of fir trees and the wet black of their trunks, with pale, dirty-white paper birches interspersed; blue smoke of the clouds, and then luminous and dark gray, the soft heavy sky billows, pulsing with incipient light above. The lake—broken branches rising here and there above the water—seems resentful, treacherous, resigned.

By the side of the road there is an overturned car, which, judging by its condition, has been lying there for some time. I see more pre-fab houses, and a swing set in the small backyard of a scrubby lawn: this could have been ours, in Jenpeg. I am reminded so much of that town, so close to here.

At Jackson's direction, Donald pulls over and we clamber out of the car. "Okay, now close your eyes," Jackson instructs, then guides me across the road to its shoulder, facing the lake. "Now open your eyes."

Jackson is holding up a photograph in front of my face. I can see the actual lake to the left and right, and he is holding the picture so I can see the continuous shoreline and a small sandy beach with a promontory of three large boulders. "This picture is from ten years ago," he says.

"Now look." And his arm drops away so I can see the shore now.

"The whole beach is gone!" I exclaim. "Those protruding rocks too."

"They're all underwater," Jackson says, pointing in the direction where the rocks lie submerged.

We continue down the road in the same direction and come to a house on the lake. Jackson shows me a photograph of the house from some fifteen years ago: the backyard abuts a small bluff with a sandy beach below. When I look up from the photograph, I see that half the yard has been eroded away into muck and weeds by the rising and falling lake.

In other places, especially along the roadway, they have put in stony riprap to try to restrain the erosion, but this hasn't appeared to work. We drive by a forested area where Jackson tells me a family once lived; he says they had to move to another part of the community to avoid the flooding. While the flooding at Lake St. Martin was the result of the province diverting water during a larger-than-expected seasonal overflow, flooding in Indigenous communities because of dams is all too common. British Columbia's W.A.C. Bennett Dam, constructed in 1968, flooded out five First Nations communities, which were all forced to relocate. Although BC Hydro settled multi-million dollar suits with the communities, this was largely seen as a compromise in order to gain support for a new proposed dam on the same river.

Jackson takes me to other places along the lake, and he holds up more pictures of the same view—from twenty years ago, then ten years ago—to compare with today. I can see with my own eyes how the water is pulling the shore apart. The lake's water level always pulsed, but it pulsed with natural seasonal rhythms. Now, as documented by the research conducted at Norway House and elsewhere along the Nelson River watershed, the more dramatic fluctuations resulting from damming have caused this widespread shoreline erosion.

In addition, logging companies in the region are clear-cutting timber to be made into lumber and sold, Jackson says. "Trees are oxygen-giving, they are medicine to the people, and they are our property and our resource. They should not be taken away from us."

At the same time, the Pimicikamak can't engage in their own forestry operations, because the timber, and access to it, are controlled by federal Canadian laws. Jackson says, "If the beaver doesn't need permission to cut a tree then neither should we."

The calm surface of the water belies the damage that occurs because of the tree roots and rocks that are disturbed: the debris must be cleared constantly or it floats out into the lake in the form of those dangerous spiders Jackson showed me pictures of; not only can they capsize smaller boats, but they are hazardous to larger boats as well, as they can break their propellers and damage their hulls.

During construction of the Jenpeg Generating Station, Manitoba Premier Ed Schreyer promised that water levels would not change beyond the negotiated limits, and this provision was written into the Northern Flood Agreement. During a 1975 press conference announcing the plan, he famously held up a pencil to reporters and vowed that the water level would only fluctuate the length of that pencil. Forty years later, in response to the 2014 occupation of the Jenpeg Generating Station and the Pimicikamak council serving eviction papers to the province and Manitoba Hydro, Premier Greg Selinger—whose deputy premier was Eric Robinson, an Asiniskawiyiniwak Cree from Norway House and a Survivor of the residential school system—issued a formal apology for the economic and social damage from hydroelectric development, acknowledging that the province had vastly underestimated the impact of the dam. Jackson

Osborne commented to the CBC, "The premier should apologize to the muskrats, to the beavers, to the fish, to the moose."

For his part, Schreyer—who went on to become Governor General of Canada—came to oppose future planned Manitoba Hydro projects as too expensive, and was supportive of wind and solar energy as cheaper alternatives to additional hydroelectric development.

What a rush of feeling had come over me when we first drove across the causeway from the airport—the golden reeds and dark brown bulrushes transporting me back in time. I stand now at the cold shore, looking out at the deep blue lake, the washed-out sky, the bright yellow grasses. "It's so beautiful," I say.

Jackson hears me and cries out, "No! Don't say that!"

I turn around, surprised.

"I don't like it when people say that Cross Lake is beautiful," he murmurs. "Because I remember what it was like before. You think you see beauty but you are looking at ruins, ruins of the land and the water."

"But it's so much like what I remember from my childhood," I say.

"It isn't," he says sadly, holding out the photographs he had been showing me. "You have *seen* that it isn't."

"How did they not know this was going to happen?" I say to no one in particular.

"It was just government people who came, and geologists and surveyors and engineers," says Jackson. "There were no professors, no biologists who were thinking about the animals and the trees."

He's right. Those who built the dam were thinking about what the river could produce, not about the whole community of plants and animals that it was the center of. They were thinking about power: water flow and wattage. How could I have thought this place was like a home to me? My mother was right: we only lived here for a few years. I had no claim to it. We didn't *belong* here. What is the connection between a person and the land he lives on? Then again, what government or document can legislate that stirring of belongingness born in the heart?

After we drive around for several hours looking at different spots in town so I can compare the views today with Jackson's photographs from through the years, we drive to a modest little restaurant in a trailer. A portion of it is cordoned off for storage. The menus are single sheets in plastic sleeves. You can get burgers, poutine, eggs, chicken strips, fries, salad, soup. I order chicken strips on salad and a cola. People drift in and out, eating their lunches, and Jackson waves one of them over, a sturdy and athletic-looking man wearing camouflage hunting gear with orange stripes and a camouflage baseball cap.

"Kazim, this is Darrell Settee. He runs the emergency services rescue operations."

"What kind of rescue operations?" I ask.

"I go out on the lake during the summer to help people whose boats have capsized on account of the spiders," Darrell explains.

"What about in the winter?"

"Well, the lake is irrational now," he says slowly.

"Irrational?" I ask, surprised by his choice of words.

"Well," he says, pausing. "It's not thinking the same way."

Darrell is talking about the lake as if it is alive. I wait for him to continue.

"In the winter sometimes the water will rise against natural rhythms," he says, "and so the ice doesn't freeze fully.

Sometimes it turns the snow into slush, which is dangerous to snowmobiles. That's how people get out to the trap-line in the winter usually. And the trappers will have to radio for assistance because their snowmobiles get stuck in the slush, or the slush actually freezes around the tracks so they can't go."

"And so you have to go out and get them."

"It's what you call an emergency," he says. "To be stuck out after dark in the woods? In the winter? This far north?"

"Trouble?" I ask.

"A death sentence," he says. "We got to get to them fast."

The lake is as much a part of daily life in Pimicikamak as it was before, but now the water has become erratic—the fluctuations are extreme, the countermeasures halfhearted—and people are disconnected from the water's bounties. The lake is an adversary now, something to contend with, and most of the fish and muskrats and beaver are gone, game animals drifting farther away, the food chain compromised. The lake itself is unsafe and the relationships between people and environment, joined for so many countless thousands of years, are now severed.

Between 1992 and 1997, the four other signatories to the Northern Flood Agreement—Asiniskawiyiniwak (Norway House), upriver from Cross Lake and the Pimicikamak lands, along with Nisichawayasihk (Nelson House), Kihciwaskahihan (York Factory), and Tataskweya (Split Lake), all further downriver, closer to Hudson Bay—renegotiated their terms with Manitoba Hydro in detailed implementation agreements that range from two hundred to five hundred pages. The Pimicikamak of Cross Lake alone refused to concede terms in a revised implementation agreement, though the community of Pimicikamak Cree that lives across the reserve border on federal and provincial land came to their own separate agreement with Manitoba Hydro in 2010, including an approximately nine-million-dollar settlement and a promise of subsidized electricity, and as part of that new agreement they incorporated as a provincial town with the same name, Cross Lake. There are some tensions between the communities, for instance while the reserve is dry, and committedly so, there is a liquor store in the provincial town of Cross Lake, right across the border from the reserve community of Cross Lake.

For their part, the Pimicikamak have been trying to enforce their rights under the Northern Flood Agreement in response to the province's and federal government's noncompliance. They began litigating the treaty within a couple years of its signing. Throughout the years the province provided little funding under the terms of the agreement, choosing to divert funds into temporary measures and continuing to litigate rather than try to settle with the community. The Pimicikamak filed their first lawsuit in 1979 and continued through the years that followed. In 1997 a follow-up treaty called the Impact Benefit Agreement was signed, but it, too, went into litigation quickly. It was not until 2016, following their 2014 occupation of the dam site, that the Cross Lake Band received a comprehensive update from Manitoba Hydro about NFA implementation and were given a new settlement that reaffirmed the original terms of the NFA and recommitted to the implementation of that treaty; the new agreement is also now being litigated in the Canadian court system for non-compliance on the part of Manitoba Hydro.

As Donald drives us back to my motel, we see a group of maybe six or seven people parading down the street. They have balloons and chocolates that they pass in through the car windows to us. They are from the Assembly of Manitoba Chiefs, here in Cross Lake to promote proposed legislation called Jordan's Principle, which is named after an Indigenous child, Jordan River Anderson, who suffered from a rare neurological condition that required constant medical attention in Winnipeg. His doctors recommended that he stay in an apartment near the hospital, but the provincial and federal governments couldn't agree on who was financially responsible for his care; during the extended time these arguments went on, Jordan died in the hospital.

Jordan's Principle, which states that no Indigenous child will be denied care for lack of funds, including for unusual or exceptional medical needs and procedures, was developed by First Nations communities in response. A resolution affirming Jordan's Principle was passed by Canada's House of Commons in 2007, but since then there have been numerous court cases for non-compliance.

In 2015 the Indian Residential School Truth and Reconciliation Commission made full implementation of Jordan's Principle by provincial governments and the federal government one of their 96 Calls to Action. So far, only Alberta has affirmed its commitment to Jordan's Principle. The Canadian Human Rights Tribunal issued its ninth order for non-compliance in September 2019. They "found Canada to be willfully and recklessly discriminating against First Nations children . . . opting to fight First Nations children in court instead of paying fair compensation." As of January 2020, the federal government has not complied with CHRT's most recent order. The Association of Manitoba Chiefs is here in Cross Lake to talk about Jordan's Principle and its implications for the community in a meeting that is supposed to happen in a few days.

It's getting colder—five degrees Celsius—and darker, so we drive on to the motel. Jackson jokes with me on the ride home: "You Americans want to chide your president because he did not win the popular vote, while we in Pimicikamak tell the Canadian politicians, 'You never won the *poplar* vote!'"

Jackson is laughing at his pun, but the joke points to a deeper truth about how "territory" is viewed culturally: rather than as topography (for military conquest or property-surveying purposes) or as geology (to delineate mineral wealth and resources), the Cree view of the landscape includes people, animals, trees and other plant life, the water itself, and even the rocks and soil and dirt as equal components. Why *shouldn't* the poplar trees have a vote?

Tomorrow, I am planning to travel out to see the Jenpeg Generating Station and then drive on to the town site, which lies somewhat beyond and, as far as I know, may have been reclaimed by the forest. I am not sure where to find the old town, so I log in to an online group comprised of former Hydro employees who were Jenpeg residents and ask whether anyone knows the exact coordinates. One of the men writes back and says that as recently as the late 1990s the streets were still there, though grown over. He explains something about the plumbing infrastructure underground keeping at least the outline of the streets visible, so I don't worry too much about finding something, as long as someone at the dam can point us in the right direction.

As it gets darker and colder outside, I turn on the TV. An old episode of *Star Trek* is playing, one where Deanna Troi has lost her ability to read minds. When Dr. Crusher assures her that many people live without one of their senses, and that her other senses may heighten to compensate, Troi lashes out in anger, saying this is something able-bodied people repeat to comfort themselves.

My heart is with Troi on this one. For a long time I claimed to be without a home, a nomad in the world. This is a comfortable lie. There were places I lived, places I cared for, and some of these I still think about. Being back in this northern landscape, walking the streets of Cross Lake—feeling the air on my skin, seeing the light on the water and light in the clouds and trees—reminds me how fully I had taken this place with me through all the years since.

So what happens when I go back to Jenpeg? What if I go back and find some trace, whether physical or internal, of the town I've always dreamed of? What then? Does this mean I've had a home after all?

9.

WHEN I SAY "Jenpeg," I mean the old town, but when the Pimicikamak people say "Jenpeg" now, they mean the dam on the river and the dormitory next to it where all the workers live. This is disorienting to me, because even if the town doesn't exist anymore, it still exists in my memory, through the shadows of the long decades between me and the boy who lived there. I find myself sad that not only might the town be really gone, but even the name I knew for it has been reassigned to another place.

Darrell Settee, the emergency rescue coordinator I met yesterday at the restaurant, is going to drive us because he has a pickup truck, which will be better than Donald's car for driving on the rough dirt roads between Cross Lake and Jenpeg. Jackson has asked if he can come along, and I've said yes. My childhood romanticism, my undefined longing for some place to think of as home, will be tempered by the presence of others. Of course, there was no way the child Kazim could ever have known that Darrell and Jackson lived not far away when I lived here in the north, so I am happy they are accompanying me back.

It has snowed overnight and is quite cold—1 degree Celsius. And since I didn't think to bring winter clothes in early May, I layer up with a T-shirt, then a long-sleeved jersey, then a thin sweater, and then a bigger hoodie on top. It is supposed to snow some more, which I am also happy about, because snowed-under is so much of how I remember the town.

When Darrell arrives, we drive to the NorthMart grocery store to pick up some water and provisions since we won't be back until late in the afternoon. It's funny that the produce in the grocery store—strawberries, blueberries—are all labeled "Watsonville, CA." These are the same berries I buy at home. Like me, they have traveled a long way to get here.

When I lived here with my family, and there was no road between the two towns, it was only possible to fly in to Cross Lake, and there were many parts of the community that needed improvements in infrastructure. Part of the Northern Flood Agreement was a commitment to build a causeway across the place where the Nelson River flows through the two arms of Cross Lake, connecting the main town with the northern portion of the reserve, which was cut off due to flooding as a result of the dam. The causeway was eventually built—after three separate appeals and the Impact Benefit Agreement addendum to the NFA—but it is now in need of repair, and depending on the season and the water levels, school buses that cross it sometimes must pause at one end, have the students exit and follow the bus on foot, then re-board, due to the causeway's weight-bearing limits, since its design took into account only normal cars and smaller trucks.

The NFA also contained a provision to fund another bridge across the Nelson River, called by the Pimicikamak Kichi Sipi, connecting Cross Lake to the dirt road that runs to the dam complex, then continuing on to the trunk road between Thompson and Winnipeg. The Kichi Sipi Bridge was similarly not built until the Pimicikamak litigated and won a non-compliance case against Manitoba Hydro.

We drive across the bridge and disembark for a moment. I stand in the middle and look out toward the island on the other side of which is the dam. This is the frozen water my mother remembered that she used to drive over for shopping trips with her friend Sophie.

The snow is coming down around us, even though it is early May.

"Some of the Elders say the snow patterns have changed," Darrell says. "Because of all the planes flying in and out."

I wonder if that is true.

We pile back into the truck and drive on.

"Have you gone back to the dam a lot?" I ask. "Did you know the people who worked on the project? I don't remember seeing any Indigenous people there when I was a child."

"There were people from Cross Lake who worked as laborers and carpenters on the dam project," says Darrell, "and there are people who work there now. A couple of engineers, I think. Not many, but some of the custodial staff and maintenance people. And one of the managers is Indigenous, but not local, he's from the south."

"Who lives at the dam now?"

"Oh, it's about twenty-five or so people from the south. From Winnipeg. They live out in the dormitory next to the dam. They were supposed to train us, you know. That's what the treaty said: that they were going to train Pimicikamak people to do the work. That we would be the engineers and the machinists running the place."

What a difference that would have made, I think but do not say. I begin to understand that the Pimicikamak are not romanticizing a wished-for return to a time before the dam; when they negotiated the treaty, they understood the potential benefits its presence offered and still offers them. And even if there are disagreements in the community now about how to proceed, they know the dam is not going to just disappear. Since it is on their land and in their water, they feel that they deserve to profit materially from the dam while ensuring genuine and thorough mitigation of the damage it causes. There have been significant material and economic benefits from this dam, including the cheap and abundant power it provides to the entire province of Manitoba, but the Pimicikamak haven't reaped most of those rewards, and worse than that, as Brian Grover pointed out, they have suffered for the enrichment of others.

"Though you're wrong about the old town," says Darrell. "There *were* Aboriginal People there. My dad used to take me to the movies in Jenpeg. Some people from Cross Lake even lived in town, including this guy who was the bartender at the tavern. And one of the cooks, Sidney Garrioch."

"Is he still alive?" I ask.

"Oh yah," says Darrell. "But he's pretty old now and he is not in the best health. Doesn't get out much."

I think about asking Darrell if he could help me meet Sidney Garrioch, but I decide not to. Would he feel like he was being confronted by a ghost from the past, a hungry ghost carrying a notebook and pencil? It feels like too much to ask. Or is it me who is anxious at the thought of meeting someone from those old days? What would I say to him? How would I explain?

Darrell points out the window at an island in the river. "That's Ship Island. The survey team first called it Priscilla Island, after Brian Grover's wife, but then eventually the province gave it an official name."

"Why doesn't the province just use the original names?" I ask.

"You tell them!" barks Jackson. "At least Jenpeg stayed with our name."

"Really?" I say. "I thought Jenpeg was named after women who worked in the Hydro office, Jenny and Peggy."

Jackson bursts out in laughter and Darrell looks back at me in the rearview mirror, smiling.

"Who told you that?" asks Jackson.

"That's what everyone always said," I reply. "That's how the story was told to me when I was growing up."

"No, no," says Darrell. "I don't know about any women who worked at Hydro, but that part of the river, where the dam is now, it's been called Jenpeg for a long time now. The original name was 'Jane-nîpîy' after an old trapper and fisher who lived out here, oh, a while back now in older days—she used to live along the Minago River, an old place for harvesting sturgeon. 'Nîpîy' is the Cree word for 'waters,' like how 'winn-nîpîy' means 'murky waters,' because that is the place the Red River and the Assiniboine River meet, and it stirs up the mud. But when they wrote it down in English it became 'Winnipeg.' Jenpeg means 'Jane's waters.' 'Jane-nîpîy.' 'Jenpeg.'"

The renaming of Indigenous places with Euro-American names is nothing new, but this is the first time I've heard of a place keeping its Indigenous name but having that name assimilated anecdotally by inventing a colonial origin for it. As I came to know later, there *were* two women in the offices of Manitoba Hydro named Jenny and Peggy, and they were proud all their lives that the teams decided to name the place after them, to the extent that their families mentioned the fact in their obituaries. So whose story is real? Hearing Darrell and Jackson talk about old Jane, I can believe that she lived here, that these waters where she fished and trapped were named for her.

The south of Canada has long had a fetish for the north, for the wilderness, which is often called "unclaimed." And that so-called classic image of Canadian life—hunting, fishing in pristine waters, snowmobiling or snowshoeing across white expanses—is Indigenous life. The act of retroactively claiming

Indigenous practices as one's own reminds me of being in the Middle East and discovering that the local clothing, music, dance, and culinary traditions were all being adopted (or re-adopted, as the case is made) by Israelis of European descent as they arrived.

The ways that the Pimicikamak are insisting on their sovereignty with regards to mineral rights, water rights, and even air rights is a reflection of the struggles of Indigenous Peoples around the world. Nominal political sovereignty through recognition of the "Band" as a legal identity has never been enough. In fact, Pimicikamak is one of the few recognized Indigenous communities in Canada that declines to hold band elections through the Canadian electoral process and instead mounts and supervises their own elections. In the aftermath of the continuous abrogations of the Northern Flood Agreement on the part of Hydro and the province, in 1998 the Pimicikamak constituted their own government separate from the Canadian legal entity of the Cross Lake Band. Under the Pimicikamak constitution, those who are elected chiefs and council members hold *ex officio* positions as officers of the federally recognized Cross Lake Band. This may seem like a cosmetic adjustment to the political mechanism, but it is a deeply significant one, since Pimicikamak Okimawin, as the traditional government is called, has now codified into written law their ancient government structure, which is a direct democracy. The elected Executive Council may only propose legislation. Proposals must be ratified by the two other traditional councils, the Elders' Council and the Women's Council, before going before a general assembly of the entire community for final adoption. Pimicikamak may well be one of the only functioning direct democracies in the world.

In May of 2003 Rodolfo Stavenhagen, the United Nations Rapporteur for the UN Commission on Human Rights came to visit Cross Lake as part of a trip to examine the human and political rights of Indigenous Peoples around the world. Besides the Pimicikamak, he also visited Indigenous communities in Mexico, Chile, Norway, and Finland. One of the main thrusts of his investigation was the engagement between local populations and the justice systems of the nations surrounding them, particularly as it related to the criminalization of protest activities. Oftentimes, as Stavenhagen points out in his official reports, Indigenous populations must resort to litigating legally binding treaty agreements through the courts, and even when rulings are in their favor, they will have to relitigate and win several judicial victories before restitution will be made. Such was the case with the Pimicikamak's series of lawsuits to ensure construction of the Kichi Sipi Bridge and other promises made in the Northern Flood Agreement.

Though many environmental groups in the United States, including Greenpeace, participated in demonstrations in Minneapolis in the 1990s to protest that municipality's purchase of power from the Jenpeg Generating Station, it wasn't until 2014 that the Pimicikamak themselves took direct action, occupying the dam site and serving Manitoba Hydro with eviction papers for abrogating their commitments in the NFA. Among the reasons for their delay may be circumstances documented in the UN Rapporteur's special report, which points out that Indigenous activists in British Columbia and Nova Scotia who engaged in nonviolent demonstrations were later targeted, arrested, and tried for minor infractions related to their actions without regard to the political and social causes for which they were demonstrating.

The 2014 Pimicikamak occupation took place after a long period of negotiation and litigation and after continued corporate and government failures to honor the terms of the earlier

2010 settlement with the Cross Lake community. Among the protestors' demands were the public apology from the Manitoba premier, a cleanup of the eroded lake and river shorelines, a substantive role for the Cross Lake Band in discussions around water-level management, immediate implementation of a program to lower utility costs for the community—which sometimes in winter months can run around $600 a month per household—and a revenue-sharing program by which residents of the Cross Lake reserve would receive dividends on profits from electricity generated and sold from their river.

As we drive over Whiskeyjack Island, which lies between Cross Lake and a series of smaller lakes the Nelson flows through, Darrell starts pointing out some of the old sites. "That is where Jane used to set her traps. North of here is where the barge-launch pad was for the Hudson's Bay Company's shipments in and out for this part of the province."

Finally we come to the dam. At the moment, the sluice gates are open and the water is rushing through. It's incredible to see a relatively small external structure, because I remember when the river was being diverted around this place and when the huge turbines were being constructed. One of the few still-extant examples of Soviet-era technology in the west, these turbines are unique because they are positioned horizontally, directly in the stream of the water's flow, rather than the more typical orientation, where the flow is diverted through vertically positioned turbines. This design takes advantage of the relatively small drop in elevation (approximately twenty feet) at this point in the Nelson River.

Right next to the dam is the dormitory where the onsite staff lives. We disembark from the truck and go up to the dormitory, and an Indigenous woman answers the door when we ring. She's a custodian in the building. She tells us that she believes the site of the old town is closed, but that if we ask at the dam's main operating building, they might be able to tell us more.

I try to contain my disappointment as we walk across the parking lot—the same one on which the demonstrations and occupation took place—to the main building and there, too, an Indigenous man—who seems to be a maintenance man of some kind, by the look of his tool belt—greets us. Yes, he says, the gate is closed at the old town site, but we can drive around that if we want. The site is currently in use by the provincial highway department as a base for its crews.

We drive down from the dam complex to the road, surrounded by the hundred-foot-tall firs I remember so well from childhood. About three kilometers from the dam, there is an access road to the left. Unlike what the man told us, the gate is actually up, so we drive through. There's a road off to the right which must lead to the old airstrip, but we continue down the road for several more kilometers, then turn onto the old Main Road.

My first reaction is not awe but dolor. There is barely anything left. The road opens into a huge clearing, where the main part of Jenpeg would have been. If there were streets here before, even overrun by forest, there aren't here anymore. The whole area has been bulldozed flat at some point in the past and is just a large open area in the middle of the forest, with a group of four or five trailers arranged in a half circle at the edge of where the trees start. There's a green warehouse building, which looks old enough to have been standing when I was a child, but that building appears to me to be in the wrong place, as if it's now in the middle of where more forest used to be. Could they have moved the warehouse or maybe they bulldozed more of the forest to make space for the various industrial vehicles currently parked around the warehouse? It's hard to tell.

Everything is so small. I don't feel any of the spark of energy I expected to feel, no sense of a homecoming.

I'd thought, besides seeing sights corresponding with actual memories, I would experience something internal, something magnetic. I thought something inside me would awaken, recognize some feeling of home. But so far, nothing.

From where I stand at the point in the road where Darrell parked, I trace my usual walk downtown. I use my body's recollections to imagine myself moving through the old town, passing first Fifth Street, then Fourth, then Third. I stand on what used to be "the Bay," where we lived, and then by physical memory cross the clearing to where the center of Downtown would have been, where the movie theater was, the general store, the tavern, the nurse's station, the men's dormitories. The distance feels shorter. Well, I was *smaller* then, I reason. It would have taken me longer to walk.

I go back to the part of the clearing that was the old downtown, and Jackson films me on his camera phone talking about coming back here, but I have no energy to describe my state of heart and mind. Jackson is so excited—he keeps clapping his hands together and exclaims, "You're here! You're home! After forty years you've come back! What does it feel like?" The historian in him wants this moment to *matter* to me and I find, inexplicably, that it doesn't. The whole time I'm talking during his recording I am looking around me at the trees, the clearing, the shed, trying to find something that looks or feels familiar.

"I'm not sure," I confess. "I thought it would feel different. I thought being here would make me remember things more clearly. I thought being in the actual place would make it more real, bring it back out of the past—make me feel like I was a little boy again. But I don't."

Jackson was right. We *left* this place. We went back to our cities and onward on the journey of our lives. And we never once looked back. This place isn't my home. It never was.

And I don't want to stay. We drive further down the access road to where I remember the beach had been, with fishing huts. There is one hut still remaining, just nailed-together boards with a yellow fish painted on the side. I walk down the muddy, sludgy beach for a while, but I am too cold to linger.

On the way back to the dam we turn left off the access road to go to where the old airfield had been. I remember the airfield, with its windsock. The tarmac is still visible but weather-scarred and with weeds and reeds bursting through here and there. There is still a windsock. Jackson films me here, as well. For a minute, as I stand there on the old runway, that flash of energy I was awaiting comes back to me. I remember our first dizzy flight up here in a twelve-seater prop plane. I remember landing, and the flapping windsock—it couldn't be the same one, could it?—glimpsed out the window as we landed.

For moments I feel bits and snatches of memories—sounds, smells—but they're fleeting, they vanish. The town that might have been the closest thing I had to having a home is gone.

The past is gone.

I tell Darrell I want to go back to Cross Lake.

After we leave the airfield Darrell turns left again, away from the dam.

"The Minago River is down here. It's where the chiefs used to meet every year. You should see it."

"I remember this river," I say, my disappointment at the anticlimactic visit to the settlement site evaporating a little.

"We used to come here and fish for pickerel and jackfish. There was a little rocky strip; the whole town of Jenpeg used to come over. There were some people from Cross Lake who came over to fish, too, but on the part of the beach closer to the road," I say, realizing as I'm saying it that the Indigenous people and the mostly white Hydro people fished in separate sections of the beach.

It also occurs to me as I speak that people from Cross Lake had been coming over to fish at the Minago River a long time before anyone from Jenpeg ever had.

Darrell parks the car on the side of the road, which feels wrong to me because I remember we used to park in a dirt lot before the forest began and then walk through the trees a little ways before coming to the beach where we could set up our lawn chairs and fish. But as we walk through the thicket toward the forest, I see why Darrell parked at the roadside. The beach is gone. Both the rocky strip and the dirt lot where cars once parked are both completely obliterated; they don't exist. The land has been chewed into by the river, and there is just the thinnest swampy margin of reeds and muck now between the lapping waves and the forest.

I turn back to Darrell and Jackson, speechless.

"There's no good fishing here anymore, anyway," says Darrell. "The jackfish and the pickerel are gone."

Standing there, I suddenly remember as a child walking on that beach toward the bathrooms and seeing an old Indigenous man in the clearing. He was staring at me. In my memory he is dressed in full traditional skins and a feather headdress, though of course that is probably a child's imagination at work upon the mind. But I do know that we looked into one another's eyes for a long moment. Forty years later I still remember the expression on his face—the calm black eyes, the prominent cheekbones, a thin mouth slightly turned down, not in a frown but in rest. Or is that the face of my grandfather Sajjad Sayeed staring back at me, mixed in the memory of a child with the face of a Cree Elder?

And who on earth did the man think the little brown boy staring at him was?

During our drive back, when I recount the story of the old man looking at me, rather than discount my child-memory Darrell says, "Hey, maybe you were there on the day the Elders were meeting. It could be that one of them wandered over to the river. Maybe you saw one of the chiefs!"

I like that Darrell never tries to guess what I'm thinking or second-guess what I'm feeling. He just observes things.

During the drive back across Whiskeyjack Island, we pass a family of black bears—a mother and two cubs—walking along the side of the road. We stop, and the mom comes very close up to the window, peering in. Eventually she decides we are not dangerous and lumbers off some distance while the cubs sit down in front of the car, lolling on the road. One stands up on its hind legs and takes a few steps toward us. Both cubs and mother are so transparent with trying to be cute for us in trade for food, their acting is nearly human.

When the Churchill River was diverted into the Nelson River to increase the flow for additional dams constructed across the Nelson on its way to Hudson Bay, there was a three-meter rise in water level. I think of the bears, the muskrats, all the individual creatures who must have lost their lives in those floods, but also think of the interconnected food-chains of other wildlife—the moose, the deer, the ducks, the geese, the rabbits, all affected by changes in vegetation—and the predators whose lives were affected by the vanishing of the land prey along with the sturgeon, the jackfish, the pickerel. Not only the town of Jenpeg has vanished: whole animal communities and nations have vanished. The nests of the grebes, which they build on the water, have been destroyed. Water-dwelling mammals such as muskrats and beavers drown when the dam is open; the debris from the spider-roots and shore erosion have ruined fishing nets and made large-scale fishing impossible.

Jackson sits in the front seat this time, because I want to be in the back, quiet in my sadness. Jackson notices my silence and keeps turning around and asking me odd questions, like "Do they have roads in India?" and "Do they have water there? Is it nice?"

I can't figure out if he is joking with me, trying to draw me out, or wanting to learn more about where I'm from.

Where are any of us from?

Darrell slides a CD into the player; it turns out to be a Pimicikamak singer named Ernest Monias, who was born in Cross Lake but who now travels across Canada performing. His country-inflected rock fills the car and accompanies us down the road back to the reserve.

We stop at an old fish-processing harbor on the road to Norway House that Darrell wants to show me. We walk across a small dirt parking lot to look at the old structures along the river—a basin where the fish waited for processing, a platform where they were butchered and cleaned, a trough that leads to another area where Darrell says they would have been packed. Beyond, the lake laps, and beyond that there are rivers and inlets, entering and leaving the lake, to make a stretch of mirrored light from the far end, which seems like it is miles away.

"This is like Kerala in India," I tell them. "I was there a couple of years ago, and you can travel from one side of the state to the other just on the waterways."

"It was the same here," says Darrell. "That's how people got around here for thousands of years. The rivers were our roads."

I remember what Mervin Dreaver told me about the "water highway" and smile, thinking of River Road, the street in Winnipeg we lived on when we first moved to Canada from India, and then I think of the ocean we crossed as a family, and the other ocean we lived by for generations before that.

"How many thousands of years? How long have the Pimicikamak been here?"

"Not just Pimicikamak," Darrell says. "All the northern Cree. One summer an archeologist came up from Wisconsin. I drove him around while he and his team worked on the excavations."

Will Gilmore, the archeologist from the University of Wisconsin, was concerned about the potential impact of the dam-related water fluctuations on archeologically significant sites. In his report on his group's excavations he wrote, "a very large number of heritage resources have already been or will soon be damaged or lost." Another archeologist, James Wright, had earlier shown that the archeological evidence across the entire area known as the Canadian Shield demonstrated a strong cultural unity. He further demonstrated consistent social interaction from coast to coast as early as 4000 BCE, belying earlier theories about the Cree originating in the east and slowly migrating westward. Gilmore's team used radiocarbon dating to determine that implements and tools they unearthed dated to nearly twelve thousand years earlier from cultures that extended across the north of Canada.

"All the northern communities were connected by water," Darrell says. "Grass River, Saskatchewan River, Kichi Sipi—what you call the Nelson River—these were the highways of the ancient world. And now, our relationship with the water is unfriendly."

"And the cemeteries? I've heard that some of them have been flooded, too."

"Oh yah," he says. "There's an old one at Ross Island that keeps getting flooded out. You're walking along and there you see—a stack of femurs, a rib bone, a skull shining among the rocks."

Then Jackson pipes up: "Are there suicides in India? Are there murders there? Are there drugs?"

Wanting to be alone in my melancholy, I don't want to answer his questions, but I realize that he's asking me because all three of these problems are affecting Cross Lake. And I remember the thing that I haven't been able to bring myself to ask anyone about: the suicides of two winters ago. One particular kind of suicide in India seems very relevant to explain to him. "Well, there's a suicide epidemic right now in an Indian province called Maharashtra. A lot of the farmers in India were convinced by the big global agribusinesses to give up their heritage seeds and traditional techniques and instead use the corporations' "disease-resistant" seeds and fertilizers and technologies. As a result, many farmers went into crippling debt and there was no recourse if they failed. Some farmers resorted to suicide, and then the worst part is that they would do that by drinking the fertilizers that had been sold to them."

Darrell and Jackson are visibly saddened to hear this, but they also seem unsurprised. I tell them too about the efforts of Vandana Shiva and her Navdanya Institute to return heritage seeds to the farmers and reintroduce them to the agricultural techniques that grew bountiful food in India for thousands of years.

96

"That's what we Pimicikamak want," Jackson says. "The same thing. We want to live the way we always had, before the Canadian people came, before Hydro."

I think of what Darrell said about the Grass River and Saskatchewan River connecting the entire North, and I think about how the Nelson River is dammed four more times as it flows north from Cross Lake to Hudson Bay. Later I learn that two more dams are planned for north of here, downriver from Split Lake, the northern-most community on the Nelson watershed.

We fall silent again, and I fall back to chewing over that old question: Why did I come here?

My time in Jenpeg swirls around me. I didn't recognize anything. I'd stood where our house was, the third one in, the middle of five on that street—where I learned to write, learned to read. The school area and recess yard must have been in the fenced-off industrial space near the warehouse; so was that warehouse the curling rink? No, it wasn't the curling rink, someone in the Jenpeg Facebook group will tell me later, when I post a picture; the warehouse is the old storage shed.

But the town I remember is gone.

Gone. The town is gone.

And anyhow the whole time I thought I had a hometown, we were living on an easement, living on the reserve, claimed by the Crown but in fact unceded by the Pimicikamak, although long-since transferred to the province's control.

And they just kept diverting smaller rivers into the Nelson to generate more and more electricity. The fight against this seems bigger than anyone can imagine, and it seems unwinnable. The chiefs didn't so much as *agree* to the dam as realize that it was going to happen with or without approval—after all construction had been going on for years even while the treaty was being negotiated. That's why, even after trying to wring every last concession they could out of the federal and provincial governments, they still insisted their white Canadian negotiators—their employees—sign the document first: they were marking the fundamental illegitimacy of a consultation process between two unequal partners.

We again pass the big signs at the edge of town with the missing and murdered youths' photographs that I'd seen earlier with Sonya, and I realize why the name Monias was familiar to me. One of the most prominent signs reads "Murdered: Austin Troy Monias," showing a boy of perhaps seventeen.

I think of a saying I heard once, summarizing the early Israeli settlers' attitude toward the local Palestinian populace and explaining how the state of Israel would be able to establish itself on Palestinian lands: "The old will die and the young will forget."

Here in Cross Lake it is the young who die. But the old do not forget.

10.

THAT NIGHT I don't want to stay in. I have been telling myself some kind of story—that coming up here, seeing the landscape, feeling the air, that somehow I would feel some kind of belonging. What I found was more difficult, more complex than I could have imagined. My family, migrants, had crossed incredible distances to arrive in this place called Canada, but the place itself never belonged to us. The irony is that the migrant is clamoring for entry into the national space of "Canada," while Indigenous people are automatically excluded from it—*have to be* excluded for that national space to exist in the first place. The further irony is that people like me and my family have more access to the space called Canada than Indigenous Peoples do because we, for the most part, are willing to buy in, sign up, and accept those naturalization papers and citizenship as if we were entitled to them.

Though it is extremely cold and getting colder, I bundle up and leave my room, which fronts on the forest, and walk around the motel to the big dirt lot that serves as a parking area.

As night thickens, the tire-textured ridges of mud freeze solid. The sky is clear and the dark is ablaze with blue lights, stars gathering together in the old stories I remember. Yet it's too cold to stand and look at them, and I don't want to be alone.

Across from the motel's series of connected trailers, maybe two or three hundred meters away, is an indoor hockey rink, one of the few recreational facilities in Cross Lake, in addition to a few baseball diamonds on the other end of town, and the skate park we passed on the way to Jackson's house. Of course, hockey equipment isn't cheap, so only some families can buy equipment and uniforms and pay for travel to away tournaments. Yet hockey is serious business in Cross Lake: there are teams for both boys and girls in multiple age groups, and men's and women's adult teams as well.

The rink was built as part of the community recreational facilities promised under the Northern Flood Agreement, but not until 1983, when that clause of the 1977 agreement was successfully litigated in federal court by the Pimicikamak. At that time, the building cost around $800,000, with construction done cheaply and quickly under a court order, intended to be an "interim facility" until a full-sized recreational complex could be completed. Yet that planned complex was never built, and an estimate done in 2016 put the price tag for construction today at almost sixty million Canadian dollars.

There are fourteen different teams that play on the Cross Lake rink; a team for younger girls is the newest, just begun this year.

Even though the hour seems late because of my travel and because it is so dark outside, the rink is busy. There are at least twenty cars parked in front, and every once in a while as I stand there another car swings into the lot and parks. I decide to walk over and see what is going on. There is nothing else to do, anyhow. Who might be playing tonight? As I walk through the dark parking lot toward the lighted building, I see a familiar face.

"Kazim!" calls out Darrell. "This is my daughter." Darrell's daughter, probably around eleven or twelve years old, waves. "She's going to practice with her team," he says as the girl hoists her big gym bag full of equipment and runs into the building. Darrell and I follow inside. "She's decided that first she's going to be a professional hockey player and then she's going to become a surgeon."

"And she'll do it, I bet."

"If God is willing," says Darrell, which makes me think immediately of the Muslim agreement to every proposal: *inshallah.*

"I've been told that the athletes from here do very well in leagues in other communities across the province," I say.

"Oh yes," says Darrell. And he tells me that the men's team won a national tournament the year before, and Cross Lake sent four women and five men to the Manitoba provincial team the previous year as well. There have even been some semi-pros from Cross Lake, including skaters drafted by the Chicago Blackhawks and Los Angeles Kings camp teams. One of their favorite sons is Jon Merasty, who played for Syracuse Crunch in the American Hockey League and now lives on the Flying Dust Reserve in Saskatchewan; Darrell says that he played for Russia's national league for a while and is coming back to Cross Lake in a couple of weeks to give a workshop on positioning strategy in hockey, called "How to Play Without a Puck." And in 2019, the Florida Panthers signed Brady Keeper, the first NHL player from Pimicikamak.

As we walk into the building, I see that most of the space inside is taken up by the rink itself, surrounded by plexiglass, with bleachers for a couple hundred people around the enclosure. The foyer area holds some overflow bleachers, with a second set of large plexiglass windows separating the foyer from the rink and main bleachers. There is a small canteen as well as a water-treatment room where townspeople can come and fill up containers with filtered drinking water now that the lake water is no longer reliably potable.

Considering the significant role hockey has played in the community, the somewhat decrepit state of the facility is surprising—never upgraded from its original layout, which was based on a facility designed for Norway House, a Cree community to the south that is now half the size of Cross Lake and was even smaller in 1983 when their hockey rink was built. Many key components are at the very end of their viability. The ice-making equipment, for instance, I learn, had a twenty-year life expectancy but has been in operation here for thirty-four years.

We sit on the bleachers next to a pair of older women. One of the women is knitting slowly, her eyes flicking between the yarn in her lap and the skaters on the ice. They are all wearing different mismatched uniforms, some in T-shirts, some in long-sleeve jerseys, and it's an all-ages group, so maybe these aren't teams practicing, but more of a social game. I keep my eyes on a lean young man in a black T-shirt and with no helmet, his long hair flapping behind as he races around the rink in smooth loops. He's faster than anyone else on the ice but he doesn't make a play for the puck very often. Every now and then he lances into the group, chasing the puck, flicks it away and runs it down the rink, but more often than not, rather than shooting, he will flick the puck back to one of the other younger boys. He's a more skillful player than any of the others by a long shot, but he's playing the game with them anyhow. Once or twice, while I watch, he will take a shot with the puck.

Other than the teams and the people sitting on the overflow bleachers, there aren't many people in the rink area, so I decide to go inside and get a better look. On the whiteboard beside the door leading into the rink I can see the times reserved for different teams and practices. The rink has been used all day, and tonight after the current practice there are more sessions scheduled all the way to eleven o'clock.

It's significantly colder alongside the ice and I am glad I brought my jacket with me.

"Can we look at the rest of the facility?" I ask Darrell and he nods and gestures for me to come along. We wander around the rink. I instinctively flinch every time a puck—or a player!—slams up against the plexiglass. We pause under the cooler unit.

"This is the thing making all that ice," he says. "You can't tell, but it's pretty old. The main chiller inside has been estimated to cost $150,000 to replace. I'm not sure how we're going to manage it."

Darrell turns and walks toward where the locker rooms are. These are no more than half the size they ought to be, considering how many teams play here, and they are dark and cobwebby. The painted cinderblock walls remind me of the elementary and middle school locker rooms of my youth, not of a twenty-first century facility.

Through the years Manitoba Hydro has been approached to expand the facility, and several administrators have come in to try to manage the facility, but each has eventually been let go due to lack of progress on having the new facility constructed. Pimicikamak Okimawin is currently considering how best to proceed. The dirt parking lot I saw outside, and the land that the motel now stands on, were all part of the parcel originally designated for the promised arena and sports complex.

We go back to the foyer area where it is warmer and sit down on the overflow bleachers to watch the game for a little while longer. The skaters are intense and intent, playing for real, with the exception of the one I was watching earlier, but as the minutes roll by, he too bends in with focus and starts scoring goals. The skaters cheer each other no matter which team scores a goal, and—especially because none of their uniforms match—I have a hard time figuring out if they are even actually divided in teams or if they are just playing around in big group.

It would have been great to watch Darrell's daughter take to the ice, but I have an early morning coming up, and I'm feeling a little better, so I say goodbye and head back to the motel. This time the *Star Trek* episode is one where Deanna Troi has gone undercover as a Romulan commander. She's acting extra tough and shouting at everyone just to make sure they know how serious she is, and to make sure no one suspects she's a tender and emotional empath playing a role that's beyond her.

I can relate. That's how I feel. Undercover. An Indian among "Indians" with something to prove.

But *what is* it I am trying to prove? And to whom?

11.

IN THE MORNING, Darrell again picks me up and we drive to the Mikisew School, one of two high schools in Cross Lake and the one attended by several of the young people who died in the suicide epidemic. I want to meet the administrators and teachers and learn about what has been happening in the last year. On our way we return to the little restaurant to get a quick breakfast and some coffee, and when we sit, an older man with steel-gray shot through his hair and a bristly moustache comes to join us. He is Greg Halcrow, the superintendent of the Cross Lake school system. He'd heard I was in town and wanted to talk, because his father had been a carpenter in the early years of the dam project.

"What do you feel is the biggest issue facing the schools right now?" I ask him.

Greg opens a packet of sugar into his coffee. "I'd have to say that classroom space is one of the most pressing issues," he says. "District-wide, we're about fourteen classrooms short, and there is no funding for expansion right now."

Remembering my experience at the NorthMart grocery store on my first day here, when I was asked if I were a teacher, I want to know where the teachers come from. Though most are local, he tells me, a good number of them come from "the outside," as he says it. One issue is that local people who want to teach still have to leave, most of them to attend Brandon University or one of several universities in Winnipeg, to do their teacher training. In the 1990s, University College of the North, which is in Thompson, Manitoba—a town of just under fourteen thousand people—opened a satellite campus in Cross Lake to provide basic higher education, including adult classes, but up until very recently, no specialized teacher training.

"We need to work on training teachers *here*," says Greg. "We just started a five-year teaching program, with twenty students currently enrolled. It's not that our turnover is big but the teaching staff we have now is getting older, and we are trying to get a jump on that situation and have new teachers to apprentice and be mentored *before* the senior teachers retire."

The new teachers are trained in a First Nations curriculum being developed by professors and researchers at the University of Winnipeg and Brandon University, and in some cases by the teachers themselves. There are two thousand students in the system currently, he tells me, in elementary through high school, but the birthrate in the community has gone up significantly in recent years, so the schools are trying to plan for the coming uptick in enrollment.

The other main curricular issue Greg tells me about is Cree language revival. Up until twenty years ago, the vast majority of people spoke Cree, but with the advent of the internet and social media most young people are not learning Cree.

"There is definitely a distinct generation divide," says Greg. "My thirty-five-year-old daughter is fluent in Cree, for example, but my twenty-five-year-old daughter does not speak even a word."

"My parents used to speak Urdu to us, growing up," I say, "but we always spoke back in English. To this day I can pretty much understand basic conversational Urdu but I cannot make my own sentences."

"It's like that here. We're starting Cree classes in pre-kindergarten now," says Greg, "and there is full immersion for all students up to grade three. The school district is hiring a full-time instructor next year to rotate through classes and teach in Cree. Right now we have four instructors at different levels, and over the next cohort's years, the instruction will track back and start earlier and continue on throughout a student's entire career, year by year. Eventually, if we can keep it up, we can have full immersion in Cree."

Although this initiative is already in process, there really are no teaching resources or textbooks beyond what the teachers themselves are developing in the classroom and what is being produced in the teaching-training programs. Next in the plan, according to Greg, will be the hiring of a Cree Language Education Coordinator to develop the resources and train teachers in their use. The current plan is for one class per grade up to grade 8 to be full immersion. "The curriculum will introduce problem solving, communications, technology, and critical thinking, all taught in the Cree language," Greg says.

Other First Nations communities across Canada are facing similar challenges in terms of language loss, but the situation in Cross Lake is doubly vexed because the Pimicikamak's refusal to concede the terms of the original Northern Flood Agreement has resulted in lower funding levels than in other Manitoban communities, like Norway House. After many disappointments resulting from Manitoba Hydro's noncompliance on projects like the promised bridge and recreation facilities, they have also declined temporary fixes, choosing instead to hold Manitoba Hydro and the province to their treaty obligations.

In Quebec, for example, there has been much greater success with language-revival programs due to significant Cree and Inuit activism back in the 1970s and '80s in response to the James Bay dam projects, which resulted in financial settlements in the James Bay and Northern Quebec Agreement;

however, an important component of the Agreement with the province of Quebec was a surrender of land sovereignty claims, a concession that created deep divisions in the community that persist, to this day.

In addition, although Manitoba has a higher percentage of French speakers compared to other Anglophone provinces—around thirty percent—they are mostly concentrated in urban Winnipeg, and across the province Manitoba's attitude toward multilingualism is quite different than in Quebec. At any rate, says Greg, there hasn't yet been a great deal of collaboration between different Cree bands across the country in terms of the language-revival programs.

After saying goodbye to Greg, Darrell and I head over to the Mikisew School, which is on the north side of town. Mikisew has approximately five hundred students, but many must repeat years, some students taking as long as five years to complete a single grade.

Principal Anna McKay, a firecracker of a woman who radiates energy, greets us at the front doors and ushers us toward her office, past a beautiful floor-to-ceiling carving of a wooden eagle with outstretched wings. Even in the short distance between the front doors and the Principal's Office suite, her importance becomes clear.

A teacher approaches with a distraught female student. "He's bullying her again," says the teacher to Principal McKay.

"What did he say this time?" the principal asks the girl, appearing to already understand the situation.

"He was talking about my mother," she says.

"All right. Get him in my office next period," Principal McKay instructs the teacher. "Don't worry," she says to the girl. "We will work it out."

"With the way things are," she says to me, "I can't afford to let one single thing go by without addressing it right away. We are still, after all this time, in a kind of crisis-response mode."

"I cannot imagine what it was like," I murmur, thinking of the suicides. She leads Darrell and me into her office and she shuts the door and comes around to sit behind the big desk, then opens a large book and makes a notation.

"It's been a hard adjustment for the community over the past several decades," she says. "In the old days, many people in the community used to raise their kids up on the trap-line. They didn't need to come into town and buy things, they didn't need jobs. When the woods were full of animals and the waters were full of fish, people could just live. The kids out there were lucky."

They were lucky for another reason: living off the grid up on the trap-line meant they escaped the residential school system.

Anna's own father had to leave his life as a trapper and hunter and become a carpenter when the game became scarce after the dam opened.

"You know, one of our major problems here is that the attendance rate is too low; out of our five hundred students, something like one hundred did not pass their credits last year. And for those five hundred students, there are only sixty teaching faculty in the various subjects. Of the seventy-four students in the senior class, only forty-six of them are graduating. There's no resident counselor at the school, and none of the counselors in the community are Aboriginal."

"Can I ask you a question about that word—Aboriginal? In the United States, we mostly say 'Indigenous' or 'Native American,' but here I've heard all kinds of terms."

"Well, the official government term is 'First Nations.' Mostly the official standard-use is now switching from 'Aboriginal' to

'Indigenous,' but most of us still use the term 'Aboriginal.' We don't know who or what was Indigenous to this place, but we *do* know that as far back as stories were told, the Pimicikamak were *here*."

"You mean the oral history of your people."

"Our memory is in the stories the way your memory is in archives and libraries. It's the same to us."

"That's why you are trying to transition to Cree language-based education."

"Oh, you know about that?" she asks, smiling.

"I bumped into Greg Halcrow in the diner this morning. Can you tell me more about how it is actually working in the classroom?"

"We are getting ready for the changes. We have four teachers. My brother is one of them. And we have a teacher who is offering classes in First Nations Studies. It's so popular we don't even have enough space in the classes. In fact, let's go!" And she jumps out of her chair and grasps me by my upper arm and starts propelling me out of her office and into the round atrium where the eagle carving is, then down the hallway to one of the classrooms. Darrell ambles along behind us.

"It's related, you know," she says. "The residential schools, the surrendering of our culture, the loss of our language, the changes to the lake and the water, the suicides—it's a long road but it's a straight one. It's led us right here to this moment where we don't know how to keep our young kids safe." She pauses. "And alive. All right then," she says, coming to a stop in front of a door and gesturing us in.

Now I have an idea what it is like to be one of the students in her care. Clearly this woman knows how to get things done.

We enter a classroom that is colorfully decorated with posters depicting Cree Elders. There is a display of the four cardinal directions and the herbs associated with each—tobacco (east), sweetgrass (south), sage (west), and cedar (north)—as well as a table by the entry with books by First Nations authors. There are several kids sitting at the tables in the back half of the room, writing homework assignments. Eight or ten guitars hang along the walls and there is a drum kit and electric keyboard in one corner. Darrell drifts over to the instruments and pulls down one of the guitars and starts plucking out a sweet tune on the top two strings.

Star Beardy, the teacher, comes over to greet us. She is a young woman, a little bit taller than I am, with long brown hair that falls over her shoulders. In a brown, fringed suede jacket and blue jeans tucked into black suede boots with fringed tops, she looks to me like she'd be more at home on a stage with a guitar in her hand than in a classroom; I really like the vibe. She recently graduated from Brandon University, where she studied Cree literature, and she is one of the people who are developing new and innovative approaches to teaching students here the history and culture of the Pimicikamak.

"I want to give them the history of Cross Lake," she says. "The treaties, the Indian Act, politics and history of the First Nations across Canada—then they will have some context of how they fit into the wider world at the present moment."

"Her classes are so popular," Anna says, "that students on their free period come in to sit and listen. Some of the kids come here to do their homework because they like being in the space." She gestures to the kids in the back.

The classes Star offers go hand in hand with the Cree language instruction offered by Kevin McLeod, Anna's brother, as they try to reestablish some sense of continuity in the culture.

"Tell me about this exhibit," I say, walking over to a corner of the classroom given over to artwork and dioramas.

111

"Oh, I'm excited about this," Star says. "It's still in process. It's going to be an oral history of Cross Lake. The students are creating their own narratives and interviewing family members using a set of questions developed by the class as a whole. The answers are being recorded and archived and also incorporated into visual representations of the history of the community."

When I ask Star about who is creating the instructional materials for the history component of her course, she pauses. "We are kind of doing it ourselves. There aren't really any, and so we just have to start creating them—moving forward."

"That's kind of amazing, Star," I say.

She smiles and looks over toward where Darrell is tuning the guitar. "You know, what I thought I was going to be when I did my teacher education was a music teacher. I still do that on the side; I teach the kids guitar, drums, some other instruments."

"How many instruments do you play?" I ask her with surprise.

She laughs. "A lot! All of the ones you see here and some others," she gestures to the instruments, which in addition to the multiple guitars include an electronic keyboard, a drum kit, and a trumpet on a stand.

"Star is one of the most popular teachers here," says Anna. "We want her to teach whatever she wants to teach."

"Music is an important part of our culture, as well," Star says, "and so I do try to include it when we are studying history and Cree life. Someday I hope that they will hire another First Nations Studies teacher so that I can transition into teaching music more, or even teach music full time."

"Can I talk to the kids for a little while?" I ask.

"Of course!" says Anna, and she and Star retreat to the desk area while Darrell continues to play the guitar. I go over to where a boy and a girl are sitting and writing homework. As I sit down at the table, the girl puts on her headphones and bends in toward her paper but the boy, small and wiry, turns to me and puts his pencil down.

"What are you writing?" I ask him.

"It's supposed to be about my summers, what I do," he says.

"I'm Kazim," I say. "I grew up in Jenpeg when they were building the dam."

"Oh yeah?" he says with surprise. "My name is Colin."

"So what *is* summer like in Cross Lake?"

"Oh my grandpa takes me out on the lake," he says with excitement. "We go out there to fish, and even though we don't usually catch much of anything, it is still so great to be out there on the land. That feeling of floating in the boat, I don't ever want to come back, but we have to when it gets dark."

"So Miss Beardy makes you write it down," I say, gesturing to the few sentences he has written.

"Yeah, she said I have to put in more about my grandpa, what he looks like, what he likes to do. She wants me to describe him more."

"She sounds like a good teacher," I say, noticing another boy sitting alone at the next table, probably sixteen, hunched down in his hoodie, his hands in his pockets, his notebook blank in front of him. I say goodbye to Colin and go over and sit down with the other student. He looks up at me.

"You're not writing anything down?"

"I don't really know what to say."

I decide to copy Darrell and Lee Roy, and I just wait.

"I didn't get a lot of sleep last night," he says then, taking his hands out of his pockets and leaning forward, stacking one fist on top of the other on the table and resting his forehead against them.

I wait.

"I'm staying at my grandma's house right now and I have to sleep on the sofa but I have to find a new place for a while."

"What's happening?" I can't stop myself from asking.

He sits up. "My ma's brother is staying there too and he drinks at his friend's place and he comes home late and gets mad and sometimes he beats on me."

I don't know what to say.

"Yeah so I'm getting out of there, I think I'm going to move out to Thompson and start training."

"Training for what? You don't want to go to college?"

"Nah," he says. "I decided I'm going to become an MMA fighter."

Mixed martial arts. Now I *really* don't know what to say. I want to say more. I want to ask him if he's safe. I want to ask him if he knew any of the kids who died, but I don't know how to make the sentences.

The students for Star's next class begin filtering in and the boy starts packing up his things into a black backpack. "Will you take care?" I finally say, and he turns to me and smiles—smiles—and for a moment he looks like any other kid I've met, in any other school, in any other town.

"Let me show you something else," Anna says, coming over. As Star begins gesturing students into their seats, Anna leads me out of the class.

"Principal McKay," I say, gesturing back toward the class.

"We know," she says, looking back over her shoulder. "He's having a hard time right now. We're trying to find him another place to sleep."

She leads me down the hall and once more past the wooden eagle looming in the main foyer. We descend a short set of stairs into another wing of the school. "This is the physical education wing," she says.

We walk through a small gymnasium—too small for five hundred students, I think—into another hallway, then she leads me into a brightly lit room with high wooden tables rubbed to gleaming and covered in knife cuts.

"This is the third component of the cultural-revival program that Mikisew is promoting. Our 'physical education' is not just gym classes and sports but includes health and nutrition as well as outdoor education. We start very early, and we teach all the traditional Pimicikamak cultural practices: hunting, fishing, trapping, tanning and leatherwork, beading, and camping. And this," she nods toward the area with the tables, "is where butchering and skinning and tanning are taught." Beyond the table there is an area with meat hooks and more meat-processing equipment—knives, bone saws, skewers, and other implements.

Along with traditional Home Economics classes, with instruction in cooking and sewing, the school's cultural education curriculum includes Industrial Arts classes, with metal working and woodworking.

The school also has a camp out on the trap-line, Anna tells me, southwest along the Nelson River; students go for daytrips and overnight trips throughout all four seasons. In the forest, teachers from the school along with Elders from the community teach them how to fish and how to trap and skin animals. They also learn hunting, in particular shooting ducks and geese, and how to prepare them. Even though there is a lack of jobs here in terms of conventional economic development, it is the hope of the schools that students will at least develop skills to feed themselves with.

All these traditional cultural practices—the heritage of the Pimicikamak—were interrupted, suppressed, and sometimes outright forbidden by a web of institutions that included the infamous residential school system and the Indian Act, which codified into law prohibitions against many Indigenous social, political, economic, and spiritual practices.

Anna takes me on a short tour of the rest of the school, which is small but very well kept, the nicest building I've seen since I've been here. They've used all manner of traditional architectural features, including sculpture and other art, to accent the environment.

While showing me the very small library, with a 3-D printer that has just been donated for technology classes, she says, "Space is a real challenge. The library is here now, but we think we may have to distribute the collections among the classrooms and use this space for an additional classroom. We're not sure what to do about the computer lab because it is already too crowded."

As Anna talks, I realize that the reason recreation and games facilities like the hockey rink or the skate parks are so important is that the incidences of substance abuse among the adult community has now come to afflict younger and younger people. There have been modest increases in funding for recreation and economic development, but they don't match the rises in population and the cost of living. The Northern Flood Agreement promised to eradicate mass poverty and unemployment with job training and education, but whatever programs have been tried clearly haven't worked.

And until very recently, the general population in Manitoba and in the rest of Canada hasn't seemed particularly sympathetic to the problems faced by Cross Lake. Economic and infrastructure development has lagged, and investments promised by Manitoba Hydro have been made only slowly, and not without court battles. Though in the original set of Numbered Treaties the federal government of Canada assumed fiduciary responsibility for First Nations, Inuit, and Métis communities—a legal principle that was a foundational part of Indigenous activists' suits against Hydro-Québec's James Bay projects—it was provincial utility authorities who negotiated with local First Nations for the rights to use treaty lands for the dams that range across Canada's northern watersheds. As with the debates about Jordan's Principle, disputes between the provinces and the federal government about who is financially responsible for remediation of the dam's impacts have caused long delays in providing the benefits promised by treaties. They're not philosophical debates: in daily on-the-ground practice they mean that Indigenous children don't have the same rights to healthcare and education as do other Canadian children.

The outdoor education and First Nations Studies classes are finally giving young people here a chance to learn and practice their own cultural heritage, which is tied intrinsically to the land. In addition to the programs in the schools, Anna mentioned the Kisepanakak Wilderness Camp, which now offers programs during the summer for youth aged ten to seventeen. Among other skills, here they can learn canoeing, including how to make their own paddles.

As Lee Roy had explained, while a portion of the Cross Lake community engages in traditional cultural and medicinal practices, including Pow Wows and Sweat Lodges, many people here frown on these as incompatible with Christian beliefs. There are about half a dozen different churches in town; the Catholic church and United Church of Christ are largest, but I was told that all the churches are well attended. Therefore, for

117

many people here, their first and sometimes only introduction to the traditional practices is in a school setting.

Anna McKay accompanies Darrell and me to the school door. "Please come back and see us again," she says.

"Maybe when I come back," I offer, "I could meet with writing students or the writing teachers. Maybe I could work with the students who are writing the histories of their families."

"That would be wonderful," she says. "And the next time you come, don't stay in the motel. We have apartments for the teachers who come from outside the community, and there is usually space." She points to a set of small houses across the road from the school.

We say our goodbyes and climb back into Darrell's truck. "That's the administrative office of the PCN," Darrell says, pointing to a large red building that we pass as we drive away from Mikisew back toward the road that runs along the lake.

"PCN?" I ask.

"Pimicikamak Cree Nation. That's where the traditional government, the Pimicikamak Okimawin, offices are. The band office in town is just for the official federal and provincial transactions; the Nation is run from here."

As we approach the road running along the lake that will take us back into the town center, Darrell says, "Do you want to see the place that the residential school was?"

"There was a residential school here?" I ask, a little surprised.

He does not answer but turns right and drives us down to a little promontory jutting into the lake. There are some houses along the lakeside, facing out into the brightly lit late afternoon. He parks in the dirt and we get out. Darrell stands, his back to the lake, looking back along the road into town.

"Where is it?" I ask after a moment.

"This is it," he says, holding his arms as if to encompass a building. "It's gone. The first school burned down in 1930. Twelve of the kids died. And one of the teachers. They re-built it, but when they closed it for good we tore it down."

So the place where so many suffered is just this—a parking area for the houses at the end of the road. I feel lost standing there next to Darrell, looking back along the road at nothing. Where do the roads of history lead? What if there's no answer to be found?

How much do any of us belong to any place? On this site, which is just a dirt promontory now, functioning only as a roundabout for cars, a school once stood, a colonizing institution where children were taken away from their own parents, and not so long ago.

I think back to the classes that Mikisew School is promoting now in an effort to reintroduce Cree culture and life to a new generation. I am reminded again of the way Canada mythologizes the "north," as reflected in the lyrics of their national anthem "The True North, strong and free!" Of course, I had realized that the activities and pleasures associated wtih the "wilderness" of the "true north"—living off the land, trapping and hunting, paddling a canoe through creeks deep in the boreal forests—were all part of ancient Indigenous life for countless, immemorial, unwritten years. These same practices were disdained and discouraged in the residential schools, outlawed and criminalized by the Indian Act.

And what does it mean to say "Canada" here? The word itself is derived from an Iroquois word, "kanata," which meant village, and which French mapmakers first used to designate the area on the northern shore of the St. Lawrence River in what is now Ontario and Quebec. It lives on in the name of a town outside Ottawa. The word "kanata" eventually came to mean the entire northern portion of the continent. As Harold R. Johnson writes, "Canada" is "just a story. It is a story that has continued for more than a hundred years, and we continue to write it. . . . But it doesn't exist in any real form. We just made it up. It is a story."

Amid all these thoughts, standing there on the empty school site, I cannot stop thinking about the visit to the old site of Jenpeg. People here believe that the landscape has its own kind of consciousness, and one can imagine that place holds memory, but I felt empty there: I could feel no trace of the hundreds of people who made it their home, no echo of our voices, no lingering trace of our energy. I think about the story of Jenny and Peggy, and the story of old Jane, the trapper. Which story do we believe in?

I think the reason I came here has changed. I once wondered whether I would be a poet here, an ethnographer, a journalist, a memoirist—but none of that feels very important today, standing on this outcropping and looking out over this ancient lake now glittering brightly under a clear blue sky.

I think of Cathy Merrick's words in that brief e-mail: "You are more than welcome to come visit our Nation." Rather than answer my questions, she wanted me to come north, not just to visit but to *see*. When the politicians and executives of the south look north, they see resources—the minerals, the oil, the timber, the flow of the rivers—and with what they consider ir refutably reasonable logic, they devise ways of harnessing those resources for "Canada," that place that by population mostly— except for parts of Saskatchewan and Alberta—huddles along the southern border. The communities that live here in the north are small in number, and in some political or economic calculus their needs were accounted inferior to the benefits of cheap hydroelectric power for Manitoba and other Canadian and American communities beyond the province's borders.

My childhood—those game-filled days and star-filled nights—came at a high cost. But it wasn't one that I paid.

On the way home Darrell needs to stop at the band office to pick up some paperwork. As I wait for him in the parking lot, I see Lexis, the boy from the Sweat Lodge ceremony, with his mother. He comes up to the car's passenger-side window to talk to me, with his strangely self-possessed affect, his quiet demeanor and bright green eyes.

"Who's this guy here," he says to me, by way of greeting.

"How are you doing, Lexis?" I ask.

"I came with my ma to the bank," he says. "How do you like Cross Lake now?"

"It's really beautiful," I say, in spite of Jackson's earlier lament that no one should call this place beautiful. And it's true, it really *is* beautiful—water everywhere you look, water and trees and the sky, wide and awakening.

"You have to come back in the summer during Indian Days," he says, referring to a big annual festival that attracts visitors from Cree communities across Canada, "or else in March, when the snow is down and all the dog mushers come."

I smile. I like the idea of coming back to Cross Lake, especially in a different season than the one I've seen—suddenly I feel the deep cold blue winter of my childhood on my skin, and I shiver. Lexis's mother calls him, and he says goodbye and runs over and climbs into their car, caked and encrusted, like all cars in Cross Lake, with the dust and dirt and muck of the road.

I look up into the white afternoon sky and wonder, what if it were earlier in the day or warmer and sunnier, could we drive back to Jenpeg?

I am still so bereft from feeling nothing at all when I was there.

Then again, maybe that is because there was never anything to find there. That boy, me, the little Indian boy gleeful in the northern winter, reciting the stories and adventures of luminous figures in the sky—he's still me, still *with* me.

We *left* that place, we grew and changed, that is true. But I lived there once, didn't I? And even if I didn't feel anything there, I have been awash in remembrance ever since I came to Cross Lake

Jenpeg—the Jenpeg that I knew—was built as a temporary town in the forest. It was built to support the building of a dam. It was never going to be there when I went back. It was never meant to be more than it was. It never belonged to us and there was nothing there to be found.

The real story, I realize, the real reason I came, is in Cross Lake. Not in Manitoba, not in Canada. Right here. In Pimicikamak.

12.

I WAKE THE next morning unsure of what to do. Darrell
has to work at the PCN office, and since I don't have access
to a car I decide to walk downtown and see if I might talk to
some of the people I always see at the NorthMart and elsewhere around Cross Lake.

My motel is on Halcrow Street. As I walk, I pass Settee
Road, then Musswagon Road. Those long-dead Scottish-
Canadian government agents gave their names not only to
people but to these streets as well.

The walk is chilly, but within twenty minutes or so I arrive
at the little neighborhood at the center of town that perches at
the convergence of the lakes. I take a seat at the table in front
of the band office, named the Chief Walter Monias Memorial
Administration Building. To the left I can see the local Manitoba
Hydro office and the bank. Across the way is another set of offices, and beyond this is a trench that pedestrians have to cross to
get to NorthMart's parking lot. Several workers come out during
their breaks from the band office and other buildings to smoke
cigarettes or drink coffee or eat their lunches. Some wander across
the street to the NorthMart where there is a little café area that
serves coffee, burgers, fries, and, somewhat inexplicably, little plastic boxes of prepared sushi, which is perhaps where Conley developed his taste for it. The NorthMart occupies the same building
that used to house the Hudson's Bay Company, shown in one of
the old pictures Jackson showed me, which the company opened in
Cross Lake a hundred years ago. Off to the right is a small stretch
of beach, and on the other side of a rise from that, the Band Hall.

A man with black hair shot through with silver, bryl-creemed back in an old-fashioned style, sits across from me at the picnic table to smoke. I decide that if I really were a journalist—and maybe the easiest thing to do is to pretend I am—I would not miss this opportunity to talk to him.

"Hello," I say. "My name is Kazim Ali, and I am a writer, and I've come up to Cross Lake for the week to learn more about what is happening in the community."

He looks up, unsurprised. I'm realizing that people in this community are probably used to journalists and government people and researchers coming around. "I heard you were here," he says.

Are people talking about me?

"I'm Henry," he says, tapping his cigarette, butt-end down, against the table.

"I'm curious to know if what I've heard is true, that there are no health facilities in Cross Lake besides the nurse's station. How do people receive care?"

"I'm the person to ask!" He says, lighting the cigarette. "I actually work in the Health and Wellness office as a medical biller. Do you want a cigarette?"

I smile and shake my head. Moose meat is one thing, sacred tobacco another, but I'm not sure about an old-fashioned cigarette.

He says, "Well, mostly for the big stuff people drive out to Thompson or else they have to fly down to Winnipeg. I am the one who helps arrange the flights and gets the money from the province for peoples' tickets. Sometimes they have caregivers along, so we have to work all that out."

"And they go out of town for everything?"

"Well, there's no hospital here. Yet. They're supposed to build one next year."

That would be the project that Chief Merrick went down to Winnipeg to raise money for, I am guessing. We talk a little more about types of cases Henry has worked on when he helps families seek medical attention in Thompson or Winnipeg.

While we are talking, Jackson walks up, waving.

"Kazim, hello! I'm supposed to go to the Band Hall for a meeting being run by the Assembly of Manitoba Chiefs Secretariat. They are the government agency that represents all the chiefs down in Winnipeg. They communicate our interests in the legislative discussions, and they help us coordinate our political responses to various issues. They are here in the community to discuss implementation of Jordan's Principle."

"Oh, you should go to the meeting," Henry tells me. "Helga Hamilton, the director of the Health and Wellness Office, will be at the meeting. You can ask her questions, too."

I agree, give my thanks to Henry, and head off with Jackson across the dirt lot to the Band Hall.

Like many of the other buildings and houses in Cross Lake—also like the houses and buildings in the Jenpeg of my youth—the Band Hall is a prefabricated building.

The meeting has been convened to discuss child welfare and the Canadian foster care system. The group that has gathered is intergenerational, but primarily Elders, with a handful of middle-aged and younger people sprinkled throughout the audience, including two young women at the far end who look like college students. There are about thirty people in all. Most of us are sitting in a big circle near the small stage, but eight or nine of the Elders are sitting outside of the circle, at long tables. It reminds me of the Rec Hall in Jenpeg where we used to go for movies on Saturdays and for Christmas concerts.

The facilitators have come up from Winnipeg where the Assembly of Manitoba Chiefs is based. Emily, the leader, is calling on people, while Jarron, a younger man wearing a shirt and necktie, uses markers and butcher paper to write the points everyone is making. The third facilitator, Vanessa, is tasked with the unenviable chore of running around the room with a microphone for whoever wishes to speak.

"How do we support the youth and children in Cross Lake?" Emily asks the assembled group.

One of the Elders, Margaret Scott, who is Lee Roy Muswaggon's sister, raises her hand right away. "Every kid is just looking at their phone. What if we had a 'Wi-Fi–free day' where all the kids would play sports or participate in sewing or cooking classes?"

I smile. Margaret's complaint sounds like something I would say to my own partner or that he would say to me.

There's another woman sitting near Margaret, older than she is, with squinting eyes and long gray hair cut sharply across into bangs, who says, "We can have Elders go into the schools and teach them leatherworking, beading, and traditional drum and dance."

When it comes to sports, everyone supports more funding for baseball and hockey, and they discuss proposals being written to fund completion of the skate park, since skating is another activity popular among the Cross Lake youth.

"Oh, I know!" says a small woman with a soft smile and black eyes, bright with excitement. "We should create a community cultural center with land based therapy. Take the people out into the woods. And you could have paintings or photographs of Elders on the wall, and offer classes like Cree language, and First Nations Studies. And it's not just the young kids that need it," she declares, taking a look around at the middle-aged and older people at the meeting, as if daring someone to contradict her.

Jackson gets up when it is his turn and begins speaking in Cree. I am not sure what he is saying, but he gets very emotional. Later I find out that Jackson is telling the group he hopes the Pimicikamak can move away from the band system completely and toward self-determination: away from the Indian Act to create their own laws separate from provincial and federal laws. He tells the story of his aunt Betsy Osborne again, how she is not listed among those acknowledged to have died from tuberculosis in the custody of medical researchers. He explains to the group that he wants to go to the cemetery with the mass grave this summer to try to find out what happened.

Then Jackson turns to me.

"OK, everyone," he says in English. "I want you to meet Kazim. He grew up over there in Jenpeg." There are murmurs of interest and the small woman who talked about the community center perks up, turns my way, and regards me with interest. "His dad worked on the dam and now he's back in Cross Lake." He hands me the microphone.

I'm surprised enough that I just look at the microphone in my hands for a couple of seconds before I stand up and turn to the group. "Uh, hi everyone. It's great to be here with you. My dad worked on the dam."

I fall silent. They are silent. Waiting. Waiting.

I try again. "But—I'm back here to listen to you. I—we—I don't think we knew what was going to happen. I didn't know anything about Cross Lake when I lived here. I was so young. But I'm here now because I want to know—I want to help . . ."

This is not going well. Why *am* I here? I still don't have an answer.

"But really, I want to *listen*," I stammer, then pass the microphone on, and look down at my hands.

The next person takes the mic and begins talking, but I can't concentrate. I keep looking down at my hands, my face burning. I don't want to look up at anyone. I don't want to see their faces and try to guess what they are thinking. I wait for a while until I feel like people's attentions have shifted before I look up again.

Emily is explaining that the report they are creating will eventually be submitted by the Assembly of Manitoba Chiefs to the federal government and the province's Treasury Board to advocate for ways of reforming the child welfare system in order to implement the Jordan's Principle legislation, which would ensure that medical and other needs of Indigenous children in the child welfare system are met in ways that are sensitive to their culturally specific needs, and paid for automatically without waiting for jurisdictional issues to be resolved.

Helga Hamilton rises to speak. Like Anna McKay, she is physically small but projects great energy, shaking her dark curly hair for emphasis when she is making a point. "The programming we can do is dictated by how we're told by the province to spend the money each month. Health Canada takes the money back if we don't spend it the right way. On one occasion we helped a family with $1,440 for travel expenses for medical treatment in Winnipeg, but we were told we had to make it up out of our own money because the federal money was not earmarked for that. What we *need* to be able to do is to spend the money locally how we see the need locally."

Many of the Elders start chiming in with their thoughts. Vanessa tries to run around the room to keep up, but mostly they don't wait for her to come with the microphone, so eventually she gives up. Jarron is writing frenziedly, whipping a filled-up piece of paper over the top of the pad and starting a new one.

"We need to have our own hospital with Aboriginal staff; technicians, doctors, and nurses," says one man.

"And the surgeons," says a woman. "Our kids should be able to go and study medicine and come back here to work."

"And we want the staff at the hospital to speak Cree with us!" Margaret calls out.

"Me and my sister are teaching the nursing supervisor how to speak Cree right now! He's doing all right," another older woman yells, and everyone laughs.

"I want to see the kids playing outside again," says the woman who spoke about the need for teaching traditional arts in the schools.

"I wish," the softly smiling woman says, "that we could have a reunion weekend in the summer where all our brothers and sisters who left would come back."

"OK," says Emily then. "Who do we enroll in the process of building solutions?"

For the briefest of moments I worry that the exuberance of the Elders will be dampened by the bureaucratic structure of the discussion, but then everyone starts reeling off suggestions for a list of constituency groups: teachers, parents, Elders, youth, volunteers, the National Native Alcohol and Drug Abuse Program (NNADAP), the Royal Canadian Mounted Police, nurses and doctors, plumbers, traditional healers, singers and artists, counselors and therapists, the Chief and council, the health director, coaches and healers, the Elders' council, youth council, women's council.

I'm impressed by the depth of political savvy evident amongst the group; I'm trying to imagine a similar level of political acumen among any typical group of Americans or Canadians. Then someone calls out "the trap-liners," and everyone laughs. I laugh too, finally in on the joke: the very people who are choosing to live isolated lives away from the community are not going to show up for a committee meeting.

The Elders go on listing the people who they think can help. It's a long, eclectic list: Perimeter Aviation, crafters and beaders, Manitoba Hydro, store owners, community gardeners, the Elder center, hunters and fishermen, carpenters, bus drivers, electricians, children. There's no shortage of enthusiasm in the community. And there aren't many illusions, either, about the challenges they face. They talk about alcohol and drug use; they talk about the social divisions in the community; they talk about the lack of meaningful youth programs and adequate local medical care. Ultimately, I find the meeting hopeful because not one person got up and left throughout the hours we've sat together.

After the group adjourns I make my way over to the two younger women I'd spied earlier, sitting at the end of the semi-circle of metal folding chairs, alongside a table. They are leaning toward each other and talking softly, with the air of people long familiar with one another. They appear to be in their mid-twenties, perhaps. One of them has her hair cut short, and she is leaning over now, plucking a long strand of black hair from her friend's red sweatshirt whose logo reads "UCN."

"Hi there!" I say, dropping into a seat opposite them with my notebook and pen. They look up and smile. "What does 'UCN' stand for?"

The woman in the sweatshirt flips her long hair back over her shoulder and says, "It's University College of the North." I remember that school superintendent Greg Halcrow had mentioned that name earlier. "We're students in the teacher education program there."

"I'm Kazim," I say.

"I'm Maria," she says, extending a hand to shake. "It's so cool that you came back to Cross Lake!"

130

"I kind of love it here," I admit, to both her and to myself. "I'm not sure why it took me so long to come back."

"Well, you're here now," the other woman says. "I'm Alisha."

"Are you writing a book?" Maria asks me bluntly, gesturing with her chin at my notebook and pen in my hand that I have unconsciously opened to a blank page.

Am I writing a book? I've been taking notes all week, almost incessantly, often *while* I am talking to people. No wonder people think I am a reporter.

"Um. I'm not really sure," I say. "I'm writing *something*, but I don't really know what it is going to be. Maybe it is just for myself. Why?"

"I just want to ask you some questions about it. I might want to write a book."

"You can!" I say fervently. "You *should* write a book, why not?" I fish around in my backpack and find a battered little business card and give it to her.

We start talking about why they chose the teacher program. Maria graduated from high school in 2011. When they announced the first round of admissions, she was seven months pregnant. She figured that since she would deliver in September, with her mother's help for childcare she could do the program. As she speaks, her eyes flash with excitement. She had been subbing already in the local school, so it was a short step for her to decide to enroll in more advanced teacher training.

Last month, despite what Lee Roy had told me about women not participating in the Sweat Lodge ceremony, Maria went for her first Sweat at Norway House—although her mother and grandmother were skeptical of whether a woman should do the Sweat. "I don't know," Maria says. "I think that idea about women not participating in the Sweats is just a holdover from Christianity—I don't buy into all the stuff about how women can't benefit or that they steal energy away from the men. It's old-fashioned. Besides," she adds, "I go running all the time, so I like sweating."

Alisha has a seven-year-old son. "He's finally in school now so I can do the program without needing any childcare," she says. She is enrolled in the same First Nations Studies course as Maria, but she did not tell her family about the Sweat at Norway House. "My grandmother would have told me not to do it. They're very religious Christians; they don't believe in all the traditional Indigenous practices."

Alisha and Maria, both young mothers, would never have been able to relocate to Brandon or even commute for hours to Thompson to continue their education; the only reason they can do this is because there is a local, affordable opportunity for higher education that keeps them within access of the essential childcare that their families are able to provide. They also both experienced a traditional Sweat ceremony not through their own families but through this academic program. I am in the presence of a community that is at this very moment reinventing itself. Maria and Alisha are also excited for the other opportunities that are opening up here. In addition to the long-promised hospital, there is a plan to develop a program for training licensed practical nurses.

"I think probably my older sister should do that," Maria says. "She would be really good at it."

What might have been possible if these kinds of initiatives had been undertaken forty years ago?

We say our goodbyes and they make their way out of the Band Hall. There are still lots of people milling around, talking, drinking coffee, and eating the fruit, cheese, and crackers that were laid out in a buffet as refreshments. A slender woman with a dark, lined face and a fabulous teased-out hairdo comes over. Her name is Merle and she wants to tell me about a documentary film I should watch, called *Sound of Thunder*, about baseball in Cross Lake.

"My grandson is in it," she says. "He was one of the young people who tried to kill himself last year." She tells me this in a very matter of fact way, perhaps because she has grown really used to talking about what happened, or because it is not at all uncommon. Or maybe it is both.

Helga Hamilton leaves the group she is talking with and approaches me. "Kazim, I am having a barbeque at my house tomorrow in the evening. Why don't you come over?"

"That sounds great! It will be nice to meet some more people before I have to leave."

"You're leaving so soon!" she says. "Listen, I want to talk more but I have to go over to the office. Some of the Elders want to go through a Sweat with the report itself before it is submitted to the federal government. I have to go and talk it over with them and decide whether it's practical. We will talk more tomorrow at the barbeque."

As she hurries away, I think about the determined resolve of the Elders that they are going to manage their way through this.

I watch Emily, Vanessa, and Jarron from the Assembly of Manitoba Chiefs packing their materials into an SUV that will take them back down the provincial road to Winnipeg.

I think of the suicide crisis, the council's declaration of a state of emergency, and the Elders performing their ritual to ask the land and the sky and the water to help. About Brian Grover writing his story and coming to regret his own work. I think of Maria and Alisha and Star and other young people in Cross Lake that I have met. After all, as Harold Johnson continued,

"The story of Canada can be rewritten. It is a very powerful story, and many people have gone to war and died because of that story, but it is a story that can change all the same."

I think about the many different ways we all got called here to this place where the lake lies across the river and the river crosses through the lake.

13.

THE NEXT MORNING is warm and sunny. What will I
do with myself today?

It's Saturday and everyone is home. There are no meetings. There's really nothing to do until Helga's barbeque later.

My motel room is small, but there is enough space on the
floor to do some yoga.

Or maybe I will go for a walk through the town again. I
get out my notebook and sit at the small desk that faces the
window. The sun pours into the room with the soft insistence
of northern light—yellow, bright, but not oppressive. Constant.

The page glows. Perhaps I should try to write a line of
poetry? But what happens when I put my pen down on the
page is a long vertical line.

Main Road.

I draw five quick slashes off it to the right.

First Street. Second Street, where our original trailer was.
Third Street, which ended at the schoolyard; Fourth and Fifth
Streets, where we rarely went.

And then I add the curve of Nob Hill where our second
trailer was, and then a final sixth slash at the bottom, down
from Main Road at an angle and then toward the woods:
Downtown.

I stare at the little map of Jenpeg drawn not based on
what I saw the other day but from my childhood memory. I
draw in the access roads from the highway. Why was there
nothing there? I try to imagine how we drove in, where we
found ourselves, and how I oriented myself. *That's not right,* I

think. *There was a turn on Main.* It came in from the highway and then it turned. I turn the notebook on its side. What if the access road came in *this* way?

Was I where I'd thought I was? I'd thought I was standing on the downtown street when Jackson was recording me, but it felt wrong. Where was I really standing? I turn the notebook at an angle and look again. The hairs on my arm rise.

I text Darrell to ask if he can drive me back to Jenpeg.

Darrell answers all the texts I send him with words like "ya," "ok," and "yup," but I'm never really clear about the when, the where, the who. The trait is familiar to me, considering the many times my own family has tried to organize a plan. You're just supposed to go along with the assumption that the other person is going to do their best and things will happen the way they happen, the way my parents will say *inshallah* to answer any question or request, or that particular Indian head-waggle that could mean "yes" or "maybe" or "we'll see," depending on how optimistic one is.

After a series of texts back and forth Darrell texts that he is on his way. The sun has grown strong, and I'm hoping it will stay clear and warm.

He asks if he should pick Jackson up, and I say no. I want to be alone, and I know Darrell will leave me to myself once we are there, and I feel like I need that isolation.

This time we drive the forty-five minutes between Cross Lake and Jenpeg in silence. I cannot stop my mind from moving and Darrell seems to understand that I am somewhere else in my thoughts. What I've realized is that I don't know precisely what Dad actually did out there. He planned out the electrical systems. Is that it? He wasn't responsible for the physical calibration of the hydroelectric equipment, I don't think, nor for any of the construction work. As far as I know, that was all done by the Russian engineers. Dad had been a young engineer in the UK, working for a couple of years in London, where my older sister and I were born. He and my mother had brought us back to India in 1972, and we were staying in the family compound in Vellore in the southern state of Tamil Nadu when the job offer came from Manitoba Hydro, so we'd moved first to Winnipeg, where my younger sister was born, and then a year later to Jenpeg.

What must it have been like for the young couple who had grown up in the polyglot and tropical culture of South Asia to move so far north, where the air was cold and they were the only non-European people living in the town? The only thing my mom had shared was that they loved the people there and that they'd had many friends.

We did have a good life in that little town. Would my dad, a new immigrant, have even thought about the politics of the provincial and federal treaties with the First Nations bands? And would any of us have even thought of the environmental implications of what was happening? Certainly the government at the time made the effort to include Indigenous communities in decision-making around issues that would have immediate impact on them, as evidenced by the consultation process during the infamous White Paper; but of course, as also evidenced by the White Paper's release, such consultation was cursory at best, and at worst was designed to give the government carte blanche to proceed how they liked while still saving some modicum of face. After all, didn't construction on the dam break ground before any treaty had been signed, and continue during the negotiations, and go on unbothered up to the actual signing of the treaty two years later?

As we drive, I look out the window at the now-familiar sight of the tops of high trees against a cloudy sky. "Do people come up this way, as tourists, I mean?" I ask Darrell, remembering what the boy Lexis had said about the dog mushers.

"Oh yah," says Darrell. "Lots of people come up to hunt and fish. In the winter the dog mushers come from all over the world, from Finland and Russia, other places too."

"How does it work for them?"

"Well, we in Pimicikamak have our own hunting and fishing rights. The non-Aboriginal people have to apply for licenses from the province. It's bad right now because there is legislation pending to give the province control over all licensing. We're not sure about that, because the federal government already controls licensing related to lumber resources, and a lot of us are concerned about over-logging happening in this area and south and west. When you go further west toward Flin Flon or The Pas, it's very over-logged."

As we pass the dam, I ask Darrell more about his emergency-rescue job, and I express worry that he is taking so much time to drive me around. They're between seasons, he reassures me. It's still too cold for many people to get out on the lake, yet all the snow and ice are gone, so people aren't out there with their snowmobiles either. He says one main project that they're working on now, in the in-between season, is setting up their own communications infrastructure, including cell phone towers and safety controls so that the hunters and trappers who move farther and farther out from the lake to find game will have phone reception to reach emergency services.

We arrive again at the access road leading toward the site of the old town. We pass the road going to the airstrip. I pull out my journal and look at the lacing of streets I drew there. I turn the book sideways and try to sort out where we are. "OK, so wait, there's another access road there," I say, and point to a smaller road on the right that I'd missed before. "I *think* we are supposed to turn here," I say, but Darrell has already gone past it. He pulls down the same road we'd taken before into the camp where the semicircle of trailers are, and I say, "Keep driving to the far end." Darrell pulls over in a dirt area beyond where Jackson had filmed me standing on what I'd thought was Main Street.

I get out of the truck with my journal. "OK," I say, holding up the drawing. "If I'm standing on the corner of Main Street and the downtown strip, then that *is* the town." I gesture toward the clearing with the warehouse and the circle of trailers. "But what if the end of Main Street is over *there*?" And I turn and point in the opposite direction. If the smaller road we passed on the main access road was Main Street it would come out here, but all I see is forest.

I start walking toward the far end of the clearing, toward the beginning of the forested area. "Where *are* you?" I say out loud. I'm about ten feet away from the trees when I see there actually *is* a road that leads up into the forest, but it's practically hidden from the middle of the clearing, so no wonder I missed it.

OK, OK, I say to myself, to calm the sudden swell of emotion. I look up the road into the forest. If I'm standing on Main Street looking toward First Street, then it should be there just twenty feet further. I start walking. Sure enough, as I walk, I can see a path ahead on the right. The road is still there! I half-run to the smaller path, a path that leads into the forest: First Street. My skin starts tingling.

It's here. I'm in Jenpeg.

Then on the left ought to be the opening of the small cul-de-sac where the senior staff, including my father, had their double-wide trailers. As I walk a little bit on I see it. Those of us who lived on the cul-de-sac called it Nob Hill, while our friends in school called it "Snob Hill." "Downtown" was where the tavern, post office, commissary, community hall, nurse's station, Mounties outpost, and security office were, as well as the men's dormitory, where my uncle lived. The trailer camp that's there now is what used to be the north end of Downtown—and past that, the rest of the town lay— those ghostly streets, still holding their outline in the forest as streets, even after forty years.

I turn from the path onto where Nob Hill should be. I can see the other end: I remember there were only six or seven trailers here. Ours was in the middle, I remember that; the Walkers and the Mollards were past us, the Van Ghents and another family I don't remember were before us. I stop in the middle of the "street." I bend and peel back some of the thick ground-cover moss. There's gravel. I lay my palm down against the little rocks.

The road. This is where our house stood.

I look up at the copse of trees in front of where I crouch. Beside it is a flat, clear area that I recognize must be the place the paved driveway and concrete blocks of the outdoor patio were. I walk deeper into the lot, wondering if I will find the plumbing outlet beneath the rise before the tallest of the pines. And exactly where it ought to be, I find it. I hurry back to the site of the house and stand there, a little dazed. *This is where I learned to look at the stars,* I think to myself.

I duck in between the trees toward the back of where the trailer stood. *This was my room,* I think. *This is the place Dad hung up the styrofoam balls he'd painted to look like the planets.* I crane my neck and look up through the once-ceiling at a cold, blue, cloud-mottled sky.

I wander back to the far side of Nob Hill and find the creek where Tommy and Donny Mollard used to catch frogs;

the place where Mr. Walker used to build an igloo each winter. I follow the creek back along Main Street. At the other end, I see Darrell's truck. He is walking up the road, looking around.

I take pictures as I walk up Main to Fifth Street. On the other side, there's a field that was the edge of town. When we were children we rarely explored this far up Main Street, I'm not sure why. There are a pair of giant boulders standing erect, almost like a shattered plinth, four and half or five feet tall and craggy. Did we play here? At these rocks? And climb up on top of them to make speeches to each other? I remember them as one big rock. Could it have broken?

The memories rush away from the remembering.

I walk down Fourth Street, remembering trick-or-treating through the snow one Halloween, that year when Flint Letain's parents bought him a horse to ride, maybe to comfort the boy for losing his brother Gus. I take pictures, even though the pictures all look the same: pine forest, open sky. But it is there in my mind, the town, the way I remembered it.

The eeriest part is walking by memory from where our old house was—just by knowing how long it took me to get from one place to another—to where the school was, where my best friend Jason Gilmore's trailer was, where our other best friend Dale Nye's trailer was, that place where Fourth Street met Main Street, and where the little hollow we used to play in was, where the creek ran, where the toboggan slope behind the schoolyard was.

I find the clearing between the trees we used to sled down—it's easy now to find that life of forty years ago: 1977, living there in that small town under the wide sky—and I stand in the schoolyard, now forested with spindly birches, where we had Remembrance Day assemblies, then look toward the school. I walk across what used to be the outdoor hockey rink over to First Street. There is a transmission tower, small, maybe no more than seven or eight feet high and no longer attached to anything. Was it always here? I have to look at the aerial pictures my family still has. Maybe Dad remembers.

I feel dizzy with time. I can *hear* the sounds of the old time—can feel myself back in my childhood body, running these streets, bundled up in the winter and stripped down as much as possible in the hot summers.

All those years I thought I didn't have a hometown. I may not have a hometown *anymore* but I'd had one once. It's here. And even though all the buildings and streets and people are gone, my feelings about the place are as strong as if everyone were still present. Maybe even stronger.

I walk from the schoolyard back down Second Street, passing the place the Gilmores' trailer was, and then the place where our first trailer (before we moved to Nob Hill) would have been. We'd run home after school, the sky already bluing toward dusk, sweating in our snowsuits, hoping to make it back before Wolfman Jack or *Happy Days* came on TV. In the evenings all the young boys my age would go to the Rec Hall for the meetings of the Beaver Scouts, wearing our little sailor hats with the down-turned brims and felt beaver tails sewn onto the back. If we worked hard enough we might become Cub Scouts someday. My uncle Turab was our Den leader and I had to work hard to call him "Mr. Sayeed" instead of "Mamujaan"—Beloved Uncle—which was what we all called him at home, even our friends Dale and Jason.

Darrell is walking one street over, easily visible through the trees in his orange hunting vest. I make my way toward him, and he hands me a scrap of metal he has found, probably a foot and a half by a foot across. "That's probably something from your Jenpeg," he says.

I heft it as we walk through the forested field to what was First Street, and that's when I realize that the circle of trailers where the highway workers are living is in the same place the men's dormitory used to be. I stop there, looking at the site, thinking of my uncle living there, wishing he could be here with me or wishing he was in Winnipeg, still alive, a jocular lion of a man. He would be in his eighties, laughing that brass-band laugh of his, keeping everyone else laughing too.

Darrell doesn't speak. He lets me have the silence and leaves me alone, walking a few steps behind me as I walk through the town and back. I wonder should I leave my little crane here? Bury it in the earth where our house stood? I wander back to the place and stand there looking at the place our house was, where we danced and put on plays, where I looked up the sky and wondered. No. I don't want to leave it here in this place, I don't want to bury it in the past. I look down and scrabble around in the earth, I find several quartz stones. I choose five, differing sizes. Five for the five of us who lived here.

I go back to find Darrell. He sees me from far down the road walking toward him and sees that I'm ready to leave. He gets into the truck, starting it up. He drives down Main Road to meet me and I climb in, and we drive off without a word. He doesn't ask me anything.

After a while, noticing the angle of the light, I realize how hungry I am, though it's only felt like minutes have passed.

"How long were we there?" I ask eventually.

"Probably two hours, I guess," he says, squinting at his watch.

We drive back across the dam. I see a worker walking from the big parking lot into the dormitory building. It's dinnertime for them, as well. This is what's called "Jenpeg" now.

Have any of the people inside the dam buildings been down the road to the forested fields? Do they know anything about who once lived there? Or have we and our lives been forgotten, just as I forgot the people who lived in Cross Lake?

When we get to Cross Lake, we return to the little restaurant, the small room with a single-page menu. We order and eat in silence. There's a man on the other side of the restaurant with the face of Conley, who I met the first day I arrived, but thirty years older. On our way out I ask him if he is related to Conley, and he tells me that Conley is his cousin. We laugh about how on the reserve everyone seems to be related.

After Darrell drops me off at the motel, I decide to take a walk and process my thoughts. I go down the road toward the nexus of streets in front of the band office. It is cold, and in my pocket is still the little orange origami crane. I finger it and think about all I have seen and learned since I have been here.

While I am passing the nurse's station there are two boys, probably in their late teens or early twenties, coming the other way. They are a little drunk, it appears, and they want to stop and talk, but I am exhausted already from the day, so I say hello and keep walking. They shout something after me, but I can't hear.

As I walk past the place where we saw the small Jordan's Principle demonstration, there is a woman coming out of a building that is blasting rock music.

"What's happening in there?" I ask her.

"It's church! Saturday night service!" she says with a big smile, jangling her keys as she walks to her car. "You should go on in!"

I peer into the brightly lit interior before the door swings shut and the music muffles. I want to go in but decide against it. I want to be alone with the water. I arrive at the small beach between the band office and the Band Hall and walk down to the mucky shore. The water glistens in wide, pearly bands. The light is deep and gray. So Jenpeg was real. I went there, I stood where it was, I let the memories rinse across my mind. Is that it then? What will I leave here and what will I take with me?

I feel lonely. Tomorrow is Mother's Day. I will fly to Winnipeg on a 4 p.m. plane, and the next morning I will fly back to the States, back to my life—this place once again in the rearview mirror.

I take the origami crane out of my pocket and hold it out on my palm. It's been with me this whole week: my witness. As I've walked and talked to people and gone places, I would occasionally reach into my pocket and roll the crane in my fingers, feeling its energy and the intention with which it was folded, and secretly imbuing it with my own experiences here.

"I can take you back with me and have you as a remembrance and talisman," I say out loud, but then I have an even better idea. I walk as close as I can to the mucky edge of the water and toss the crane lightly into the lake. I release it into the water. I want it to float off and then sink, become part of the lake as I pray for the future of Pimicikamak and for myself. A gull flies down and plucks it up and drops it again. And then swoops again, plucking it up for a moment and dropping it. It floats farther from shore. I have to squint a little in the fading light to keep it fixed in my vision. It is far out there. It hovers there, light, glowing orange in the lengthening light.

I imagine the gull as a spirit coming down and blessing the crane.

It hovers.

Then slowly, very slowly sinks.

Then the water takes it in.

The sun is bright and cold.

It disappears into the lake.

I walk back. There's a message from Helga saying the barbecue had to be postponed because she was late coming back from Thompson. She invites me to come to the Band Hall tomorrow for a community Mother's Day breakfast given each year. I phone back and say I will come, but only if I can volunteer to help. She will tell the caterer to expect me.

Tonight I can't fall asleep in the motel room. I pull up the comforter and all the pillows into the center of the bed and make a womb-like space to crawl into. I put on a CD of Sheila Chandra's drones, which fill the room, and I pull my knees up into my chest in a fetal position and lull myself to sleep.

I wish there was someone from my old life here, someone to talk to. About being the "other kind" of Indian, both kinds wearing a name given to us by outsiders, names to which we do not belong. Who could I explain this to? How strange it feels to be a stranger myself. Returning to the scene of the crime.

I close my eyes against time. I can still hear my childhood pealing in my ears.

14.

I PACK MY suitcase and leave it in my room then walk through the town again, now familiar with the winding streets, I go into the Band Hall, which looks so different from the other day, during the meeting on child welfare. Now there are decorations, pink flowers on the tables, and the tables are all in long rows. At the far end of the room, near a small kitchen area with a pass-through, an imposing woman with long curly hair coiled into a high bun is issuing orders to a small group of volunteers. I approach.

"Hi, I'm Kazim Ali. Helga Hamilton sent to me to volunteer with you."

"Oh, good," she says. "We can use the help. I'm Deeja. We're going to have something like four hundred people in and out during the course of the morning, so we have to hustle to get the place settings ready."

We lay out salt and pepper shakers and small styrofoam plates piled with cold butter pats. I help to set up the food stations along the walls—there are all different kinds of eggs, toast, waffles and pancakes, maple syrup, various types of potatoes, ham, bacon, sausage, cheese, and fruit. The other volunteers and I each take food stations to serve. I end up with the job of serving the ham slices, sausage, and bacon.

It's a little funny to me, being the Muslim vegan serving the breakfast meat, but I'm actually looking forward to seeing all the women who will come through. I've been here for a week but I've only seen a few people at a time. As soon as they open the door, women of all ages start coming in, some in groups of two or three, and others in large crowds. They are laughing and joking with each other, and soon the hall is filled with a festive air. The women line up and come through the line, choosing pancakes or waffles, boiled eggs or poached, scrambled eggs or fried, hash browns or home fries.

Everyone is happiest when they come to my station, and I can barely keep up. Some people want all three meats, some people want ham more or sausage more, but *nobody* says no to the bacon. In the beginning I try to be conservative so I can make sure not to run out, but after several rounds of the women insisting on another piece or two, I start doling out more generous portions. True enough, when one pan empties, there is another from Deeja. We settle into an easy rhythm of serving, and the room fills with that sound I remember so well from our family homes in Winnipeg: women talking loudly to be heard over one another's laughter.

At some point, about an hour in, there is a stir near the door. I peer through the crowd to see who has entered. It's Cathy Merrick, dressed in the long traditional skirt with embroidery at the bottom that I see many of the other women wearing. I'm glad she's back and wonder how her meetings in Winnipeg went. I watch as she begins at the end of the long table nearest the door and goes one by one around the room hugging each woman, stopping and having a short conversation with her and then moving on to the next woman. When she has gone the length of one long table, she saunters over to the next. Once she has made her way around the whole room she comes to the serving tables where the volunteers are, and spends a few minutes chatting with each one, sometimes just a word or two, but she is sure to spend time with every person.

When she comes over to me, she smiles a mischievous little smile, and suddenly I imagine I'd be able to recognize a picture of her as a little girl.

"And how has your time been in Cross Lake?" she asks.

"It's been wonderful," I tell her fervently. "I want to tell you all about it!"

She comes around the table, takes me by the shoulders, and gives me a hug. "After the breakfast is over, I will take you back to the motel to get your suitcase, and then we can go to my house to chat. Then I'll drop you off at the airport for your flight. How does that sound?"

I nod agreement.

"I'm sorry I couldn't be here while you were here. I've been in Winnipeg all week in meetings about the new hospital, trying to get the province to contribute more resources."

"What can I do to help?" I ask.

"Do you have twenty million dollars?" she shoots back, with a smile.

She continues along the line, greeting the volunteers and the mothers. My phone vibrates in my pocket. There is a message from Darrell: "are you at the airport". . . I text him that I am still in Cross Lake, at the Band Hall. He writes back, "ok be there in 30 minutes." I'm touched that he wants to say goodbye.

Lee Roy's sister Margaret, who I'd seen at the meeting here in the Band Hall, appears. Margaret has strong features and probing eyes. She is wearing a long traditional skirt, like the one Chief Merrick is wearing, but unlike the Chief's staid blue, Margaret's skirt is a hot pink and the embroidery is turquoise and dark green.

"Chief Merrick has told me about you!" she says. "Will you pronounce your name for me?"

I pronounce "Kazim," and she ambles over to the far side of the hall, where there's a low stage with a microphone, which Margaret takes in hand.

"Hello, mothers," she says, calling their attention. The room quiets down and they listen as Margaret switches between English and Cree throughout her speech.

"We're lucky to have a guest with us today," she says, "His name is Kazim Ali and he is a journalist from the United States." I tense up a little, wanting to correct her, but then I relax again. Maybe I *am* a journalist. Or maybe what I am is something different, something that can't be explained so easily. Margaret goes on, "He grew up here. He grew up in Jenpeg." She gestures off behind her, toward the lake. "His father was one of the workers on the dam."

There is a titter of interest through the crowd. My skin starts prickling. What will everyone think? It's true, I've told this to people one on one, and Jackson told everyone at the Jordan's Principle meeting, but now I am in front of what feels like the whole community.

"He's come back," says Margaret. "He wants to know what has happened with us in Pimicikamak since they built the dam. Welcome him."

I wave to the crowd, smiling weakly, and then all the assembled mothers begin to applaud. "Thank you for coming back!" one of the women shouts out as the other women cheer. "You came home at last!" another one yells from her seat. "We've been waiting for you," says the elderly woman over whose plate my tongs quiver with a thick slice of ham.

From then on, all the women coming through the serving line ask me how I like Cross Lake, have I been back to the dam yet, how is my father doing these days, whether my father is going to come back and visit them too. There's no sense of reproach or resentment in any of these interactions. I am too overcome with emotion to make anything but courteous yet cursory responses. I bend my swelling emotions into my small task of serving the bacon.

After a while, we move what's left of the waffles and pancakes and other savory foods to one end of the table to make room for trays of fruit and cheese, pastries and chocolates, and urns of coffee and tea. The women are milling around, talking, saying goodbyes; some men have shown up with the children. While the girls and younger boys reunite with their mothers and grandmothers and gorge on fruit and chocolate, the few men who are here—just three or four of them, and a pudgy teenaged boy in a Toronto Maple Leafs sweater—busy themselves with clearing plates from the tables and cleaning the hall. One of the men is wearing a jersey for the Cross Lake baseball team, which is called the Braves and uses the same logo as the Atlanta Braves. Let's see someone try to sue them over that.

Margaret has slid off her pink skirt; she was wearing gray sweatpants underneath the whole time. She is walking around talking to everyone, the skirt slung over one arm. I like her even more.

Many of the women come by to talk to me, to ask me about where I've been since I left Jenpeg, what I've been doing; they ask after my mother and father.

While I am packing my notebook and pen into my backpack, I spot Darrell in the crowd. He comes over to say goodbye. He wants to give me some of the education materials and reports he has done on land surveying and infrastructure.

It feels strange to take my leave of him. He is the person who spent the most time with me throughout the week and shared the most with me—about his family, his aspirations for the renewal of the Pimicikamak. I think of the moment when I was talking to Star, the First Nations Studies teacher, in the classroom at Mikisew, and he drifted to the back of the room and found a guitar and began plucking away, finding the lightest and sweetest notes. He was always nearly invisible—each day hovering at the edge of my conversations.

As we part, Darrell and I shake hands and he says, "God Bless."

15.

AS THE PARTY winds down, Chief Merrick introduces me to Janice McKay, the organizer of the event. Her family moved to Cross Lake from Norway House. Her father was the Chief of Norway House who signed the Northern Flood Agreement.

"What do you think your father would say if he saw how everything turned out?" I ask her.

"Well, when the Agreement was signed," she tells me, "things were already complicated and difficult for the local people. They were contending with hundreds of years of history that had taken so much from them. I think they saw the Agreement and the dams as lifesavers that would help turn things around. Like they finally had something to bargain with. And I don't think they felt they were truly going to be able to stop the dam from being built anyhow. It felt inevitable, I guess."

Chief Merrick adds, "Some people say the chiefs had no choice but to work with Hydro and the province. I do think that at the time they thought this was the best chance for their communities."

We say goodbye to Janice, and Chief Merrick and I make our way to her pickup truck, which is parked outside, the same one Sonia used to drive me in, on the first day. We drive across the road to the NorthMart because she wants to get a few things. Once inside, she stops at the cut flowers section and chooses a bouquet. There is a special on china teapots, and she has a brief discussion with the stock boy about which are on sale and which are not. It turns out she has a collection of teapots, and there is one here she doesn't have, English style, with a baroquely thick profusion of painted flowers. I think of the more Asian-style teapots Marco and I buy from the potters in Oberlin and wonder how well I would have to pack one to survive the journey north if I were to try to send one to Chief Merrick.

I take her groceries out to the car while she and the clerk pack up the teapot in a small box with a little crumpled-up paper as buffer.

In the parking lot, a car flashes its lights at me. I walk over to the black SUV and see that the driver is Lee Roy. The rest of the car is filled with teenaged boys.

"How was your week?" Lee Roy asks, extending his hand, which I shake.

"I can't believe it has only been a week. It feels like much less than that and much more, all at the same time. I want to come back when the weather is warmer. Will you take me out on the water in your boat?"

"Sure I will. Do you want to go hunting?" he asks. "Find a moose?"

I smile. "We'll see. Where are you heading?"

"I'm driving the boys to their baseball tournament," he says, smiling the first smile I've seen on him. "We have seven hours to drive." The boys wave. I wave back.

"Good luck to all of you," I call to them, rapping on the side of the car for luck.

Lee Roy holds his arm out in farewell as they pull away. "Come back and see us again," he calls back.

"I will!" I shout, but I don't know if he hears me.

Chief Merrick comes out with her box, and we drive first to my hotel, where I bring out my suitcase and heft it up into the truck bed, and then her house. She lives here with her husband; her older son, his girlfriend, and their son; her younger son; and her brother. Until recently when she passed away, her mother had also lived with them. I express surprise at so many people in a normal-sized house, but she confirms what Sonia told me earlier, that some houses of the same size have ten to fifteen people living there. The winters are so cold that housing and heating is critical; there is no—can be no—"homeless population," though there are people who do not have homes of their own and live with others, like the boy I met at Mikisew, and there are those who have moved to Thompson or Brandon or Winnipeg, because there is no place to stay here.

While I help her put away groceries, Chief Merrick unpacks the teapot and shows me the others, displayed on shelves in the kitchen and along the tops of the cupboards. I ask her if she just collects teapots or if she actually uses them all, and she exclaims, "Of course I do!" with something akin to girlish delight. She puts the new one up above and brings another one down, blue with a light starry design, to make tea.

Her grandson Kingston is playing video games in the living room, and she asks him to go to his bedroom so we can sit and talk.

"I want to know who Cathy Merrick is," I say. "And how did she become the Chief of Pimicikamak?"

She smiles and begins recounting her story. Her parents were from Cross Lake, but she grew up outside of Winnipeg. When she was a very young girl, around two years old, she was removed from her birth family, in the "Sixties Scoop," because her parents already had several children and the Canadian social worker deemed them unable to care for another child. She was given to a white foster family to raise. Cathy Merrick's foster family lived in Steinbach, a small city, southeast of Winnipeg. It wasn't until she was around nine that her foster parents took her north to Cross Lake, where her birth family had since returned. They went intending to complete the formal adoption process, but on the visit it became clear that her birth family wanted her to remain with them; her foster family relinquished her. Eventually, like many other Indigenous children, she was required to go through the residential school system and later went to the university in Brandon. When she completed her studies, she returned to Cross Lake. Throughout her childhood and young adulthood she stayed in touch with her foster family and maintains a relationship with them to this day. "I have two mothers," she says without bitterness, "and two fathers."

When she came back to Cross Lake after her university studies, she worked in several different capacities for the band, at first as the Associate Health Director of the Cross Lake Band and later as Executive Director, overseeing all the band's business, finance, and administration. Her experience in this role made her want to go into politics, and she served on the executive council for twelve years, including under Chief Walter Monias. She ran two unsuccessful campaigns for Chief, and was considering whether to run a third when she decided to meditate and pray.

"I said, 'Creator, show me where you want me to be,' and I resolved that if I lost the third election, I would resign from politics and find another way to serve the community."

"Those twelve years on the council must have been challenging," I say, "if you were one of the few women in politics."

"Oh, yes," she says with conviction. "There had never been many women on the council even though there had once been a woman Chief back in the old days. All those men used to call me 'little girl' as a nickname. They meant that with affection, but it cut both ways."

"What do you feel are the most pressing issues facing you as Chief?" I ask.

"It's getting this hospital built," she says decisively. "There is no comprehensive hospital in Cross Lake, only the nurse's station, staffed by a nurse and some emergency medical technicians. They want to give me a million dollars for an interim center, but I am worried about accepting any temporary measure."

I think about the "interim" hockey rink, thirty-five years later, and think she is probably right to worry.

"We're going ahead with our plans," she declares. "We have already begun a doula training program with Aboriginal women, and the licensed practical nurse courses begin in September. We have thirteen nurses for the first class, six of them from the community and seven from outside."

She retrieves a tube from a desk in the corner and pulls out the blueprints for the hospital, unrolling them on the coffee table between us. She starts pointing at the different facilities and explaining.

"There is no blood lab here to do blood work now, and there's no prenatal or neonatal care available here."

"Really?" I say with some surprise.

"Every pregnant woman has to leave the community to give birth. At least if we have trained doulas, a woman could choose."

She pauses and looks down at the table and then out the window and then back at me. She looks into my eyes.

"Birth is the crisis," she says. "Thompson is where the clos-est comprehensive medical services are. It's three or four hours from here, lots of that over dirt roads. Pimicikamak mothers give birth there, then return here. If there are any predicted complications, they may even have to go to Winnipeg to give birth. There's no balance between life and death here in Cross Lake," she says. "I want babies born in this community."

Kingston comes back into the living room and begs her to let him watch his favorite show on TV. "Grandma, it's a *science* show!" he says. I smile, and she nods her permission..

We go back to talking about the hospital. She says it will include centers for traditional healing and integrative medicine, as well as operating rooms, X-ray machines, and other kinds of diagnostic equipment.

There are, of course, more challenges to the community's health and wellness, not the least of which is the very real problem of substance abuse.

"That bar and the liquor store at the edge of town," she says, "are on provincial land. We are trying to get them closed as a threat to public health, but so far without luck. Before, until 1969, it was a federal law that if you drank alcohol you would lose your Treaty Status and not be allowed to go to university. It's different now."

I want to ask about the paternalistic nature of laws like that, but I don't feel like it's my place. Instead I ask about the signs on the edge of town, the ones showing the faces and names of missing and murdered youth.

Chief Merrick gets a canny look on her face. "I'm the one who put them up," she says. "These are young people, victims of violent crimes that are unsolved. Because the community is so small and so many families stick together, there can sometimes be a cult of silence."

Some of the "missing" may be dead. There are rumors, or rumors of rumors: they've been killed in a fight or hunting accident or car accident, and their bodies were taken out somewhere and buried secretly.

"I want us to confront this issue," she says. "I don't want anyone to be able to avoid thinking about these young people.

That's why the signs are at the edge of town, so everyone coming or going will see them."

There has been criticism of the signs directed at Chief Merrick. Some feel that the signs present a bad side of the community. Others criticize her for working too closely with provincial officials. As in any vibrant democracy, there is disagreement within the community about the best way forward, the best way of dealing with Manitoba Hydro and the province, and some lingering differences around people like Cathy Merrick who have strong connections off-reserve and in Winnipeg. There is one other thing: the Dakota man, the one who is one of the managers at the generating station, is Cathy Merrick's husband.

"Yes," she says, laughing. "We've had some fun dinner conversations! I had to lead the occupation against him." We laugh about it, but the situation does point to the complexity of the various interconnections and interrelationships between the people of Cross Lake and the Jenpeg dam. She stops laughing and becomes pensive. "It has been difficult," she says. "I go down to Winnipeg a lot. To talk to the province. To get money. It's my job. But there are people who say I should be staying here more and taking care of the people here. It's a balance I have to keep."

"It must be difficult," I say.

Though we were both at the brunch all afternoon, neither of us was eating, so when she asks if I am hungry, I say "Yes!" with some gusto. She gets up and goes to her cupboard and pulls out some cans of corned beef hash. I don't say anything. A week of non-vegetarian/non-vegan food has been playing a little havoc with my system, but when the head of a government in whose territory you are currently sitting is standing at her stove in her house shoes frying you up a plate of corned beef hash, you say: "Thank you, ma'am." And you mean it.

As we eat, we talk of the major ironies of the Northern Flood Agreement. Cheap electricity was promised to the community. Manitoba Hydro was supposed to provide subsidized power to Cross Lake at a cost of $8 per month, but this has not been honored; in fact the utility bills are scaled much higher here. And even the compensatory agreements made after the 2014 occupation have not been abided by.

And then Chief Merrick makes the observation that allows me to finally understand everything: why the provincial government and Manitoba Hydro are so stingy, why the people here sometimes say the company is trying to starve them out, encouraging them to leave—the one reason the authorities will not undertake the economic development that would make this community viable.

She tells me, "We are sitting on top of a giant source of titanium, but we refuse to sign any mining agreements. They want to develop an open pit mine with a thirty-thousand-ton-per-day capacity, but we retained all of our mineral rights under the NFA and we won't surrender them, even if the provincial town of Cross Lake has."

"I don't blame you for not allowing mining," I say. "If you thought the dam was bad, just wait until they start mining up here!"

Natural gas and oil as well as the minerals and metals of the Canadian north provide a significant portion of Canada's wealth. Titanium, in particular, being both lightweight and durable, is sought after for use in aircraft and spacecraft hulls and engines, ship hulls, and for laptop computer and other electronics production. In the coming decades, all their fresh water is going to be a hot commodity too, I think, not only as drinking water but also because fresh water is vital to the silicon production that is at the heart of the electronics industry. And if the infrastructure were created and the government took control of resource licenses, there would be huge potential from the tourist industry to cater to people from around the world interested in wilderness expeditions, in hunting and fishing and in hiking or camping. In addition to that actual motherlode of titanium, the Pimicikamak are sitting on the proverbial gold mine.

"Oh!" Chief Merrick says then, catching sight of the clock on the shelf. "We should start getting ready to leave. The airport is only a ten-minute drive from here, so we're in good shape."

I gather my things, and she goes to get her purse and keys.

"It has been so wonderful to be here," I tell her. "I've been making a list in my head of all the things I want to do when I come back. I never got to go out on the lake like I wanted too because it was a little cold."

She smiles. "What else do you wish you could have done that you didn't have a chance to do?" she asks me.

"Well," I say, "for one thing, when we were kids, my mom and her friends would drive over to Cross Lake and then come back with all kinds of things: jackets and fur-lined gloves and mukluks. I wish I had a chance to meet some of the traditional crafters and beaders and tanners, and watch them work, and be able to buy some of their crafts."

She smiles and puts a finger up to tell me to wait, and she disappears into one of the bedrooms. I hear her rummaging around in a closet or chest, and when she comes out she is holding a pair of moccasins.

"Try these on," she says, and I do.

"They fit perfectly!"

"They were made by my aunty," she says. I love the little red and white pattern beaded into the tops. As I walk around the room I can see how comfortable they would be for walking in the yard or on an earthen path.

I thank her and pack the moccasins carefully in my backpack, and we go out to her pickup truck. As we pull out onto the road, she flips on the radio and starts singing along with a Jesus-inflected country song—by now I recognize the smooth, warm voice of Ernest Monias—and lights up a Canadian Classics cigarette.

I take a chance and ask her what her own religious convictions are and what she thinks of divisions in the community around religious and spiritual practices. She says she still belongs to the United Church of Christ and goes occasionally. I ask if there is tension around the fact that she is one of the people trying revive some of the old ways.

"Well," she says, "a lot of people feel like they have to choose one or the other, but are they really exclusive?"

"What do you mean?" I ask.

"The Indigenous law and being is first and foremost for us. In how we treat the land, and how we live in connection with it and with the community as a whole. But as to how we live with one another, there are many different ways and views."

The divisions and cross-pollinations of spirituality are historic to the Pimicikamak. Back in the 1700s when they were first encountering French and, later, English missionaries, the Indigenous community at Norway House mostly became Christian, while the community at Cross Lake resisted the missionary presence, refusing them permission to build a church there, and continued their own traditional spiritual practices, led by medicine men like Tespastenum.

The encounter between Indigenous Peoples and settlers has always been dynamic, with many of the leaders of the past trying to strike the balance between holding on to the ways of community and trying to survive in the new political reality of an invasive and unrelenting colonial European presence.

162

The old medicine man Tepastenum for years refused to embrace Christianity but his wife and children were all baptized; this mixed-faith family structure perhaps reveals a historic pluralistic worldview deep within Pimicikamak belief systems. For his part, when it came time to go meet with the Crown representatives to discuss Treaty 5 he quickly underwent baptism. Having always been known by the traders and missionaries to reject Western hairstyle and dress, he stunned the Crown representatives by appearing at the conference with his hair bound up, wearing a Victorian suit and necktie, and calling himself Daniel Ross, the Christian name he had been given at his baptism. Like the other Indigenous leaders present he signed the document with the single letter X, and upon his return to Cross Lake, he dispensed with the suit-jacket, waistcoat, and pants, and once more donned his own clothing, unbound his hair, and used his own name.

"So, I want to tell you about a ceremony that I did," I say slowly to Chief Merrick.

"Oh!" she exclaims with that child-like delight and mischievous smile I have grown to enjoy so much. "What did you do?"

I explain to her about the crane I brought with me, which I'd held in my pocket all week long. I tell her how I took it to the lake.

"And then you let it go!" she completes my story.

"I let it go into the lake."

She smiles wordlessly, her eyes on the road. She reaches out and takes my hand and squeezes it. Ernest Monias croons on.

At the airport we embrace. I say, "I am taking you with me. I won't forget Cross Lake."

She says, "We are a part of you now. You left a part of yourself with us, remember? We will always have a place for you here."

16.

I'M IN THE plane now, we are preparing to depart. Rain sluicing down the window. Bear me south safely, I pray.

I listen. I hear.

I write in my notebook a little poem:

The lake ridden land, river riven
Soaked and silky with silt
The water-born and water-borne—

*

Evening. Winnipeg. It is so strange to be back in a city, amid the concrete and steel and glass after my long week in the north. The sun casts shadows in the late afternoon.

I arrive at the airport and go straight to the car rental place and jump into a car and hit the road. I have a pilgrimage to make.

I drive through the streets. I am following my GPS to a place I have not been to in thirty-eight years. Nothing is familiar to me, not until I pull onto the wide divided road that runs by the Canadian Mint. Past the Mint a little bit and to the left is the driveway I want.

I pull into the main entrance to the cemetery and follow the directions my cousin Saira sent me. I drive around the perimeter road to the garden shed. Just on the other side is the Muslim section. My grandfather—who died in 1980—and my uncle—who died in 1984—were among the very first buried in this part of the cemetery. When we came to bury my grandfather, none of the other stones were here yet. There wasn't even grass yet. It might have even become the "Muslim section" because his grave and that of my uncle were here.

I take a walk through the section, looking at the names of others who have lived and died here since then. There is a young man buried here named Adam Gamel, born in 1971, the same year I was, but who died in 2003, and a little further on, there is a stone for a baby with the last name Bokhari, whose dates were June and October of the same year. We must have known that family; they must be related to the Bohkaris we knew growing up.

When I see that Bokhari stone I realize that our names *are* here in Winnipeg, and that the Muslim community is big now. There is a whole section in the cemetery: we are leaving our dead among others.

I pace up and down, but I cannot find the stones of my uncle and my grandfather. After two passes, I see they are right at the beginning, so close to the tree and the shed that I missed them and kept missing them.

The sun has lengthened even further. The light is dark yellow. My grandfather's and uncle's stones are covered with last winter's detritus. No one has been here to clear them. I do my best to clear away the muck and decomposed leaves. I uncover their names. *Mohammed Sajjad Ali Sayeed. Turab Ali Sayeed.* I sit with my uncle and my granddad as the sun goes down.

At some point, I start talking. I tell them about the family. I tell Mamujaan about Tanvir, his son who lived apart from the family for many years and about Tanvir's two sons, his grandsons. I tell him about how Saira married and moved to California, and from her he has three granddaughters and another grandson. I tell him how his granddaughters have all graduated from college, and his grandson, too. The youngest granddaughter is a vegan like me and an art lover, too.

I tell granddad how amazing it was he raised five strong girls, my mom and my beautiful aunts. That my sister Naheed's daughter and my sister Farrah's daughter are just like them. How strong they are. How many places they will go.

I say to them, "I have just been to Jenpeg. I have just gone to Cross Lake." I tell them about the people there, about the waters and the sky.

Time passes. The sun gets lower. Eventually I run out of things to say and just sit. When will I be able to come back here? There is a trauma in leaving our dead in the earth so far away. We've left our ancestors' resting places all over the world, and we don't even know where they are. Every once in a while a cousin from Pakistan will visit the cemetery in Karachi and send a photograph of one of our grandparents' graves, but for ancestors older than that generation, I only know a few names, and I wouldn't even begin to know where they lived or died.

Where are the histories of our people written into the land? Are we landless people?

We are not landless people. We will always belong to the place we buried our ancestors, where we came into language and learned to write, where we first prayed to God and looked up at the infinite sky.

We belong to the places of our earliest griefs, belong to where we left our dead, and belong to places where those younger than us were born.

And then in my ear I hear the screams of my mother that tore through our house that long-ago summer when we got the phone call from faraway Winnipeg that her father had died. And then again only a few years later—another call, when her brother had died.

I have wandered the streets of Jenpeg, the town where my earliest memories were, where I came into language, where I first looked up at the dark sky and saw the galaxy of stars. Where I learned the myths that told the names of those frames of light. Where still echoes the great booming voice of my uncle, Turab Sayeed, one of the greatest heroes of my heart.

Am I from a place? I have one card that says I am from California, but I have only lived there a little while. I have a blue book that says I am from the United States, but I have another paper that says I am Canadian and another that says I was born in the United Kingdom. And what of the home of my parents and grandparents and great grandparents, what about India?

What does it mean to be "from"? What do I think of when I think of "home"?

After all these years of thinking otherwise, all the continents and countries I have wandered, of the many places I have felt "from," the one that feels strongest is Jenpeg, a little town a few kilometers away from where the river is dammed—a little town in the forest that existed once and always will.

Places do not belong to us. We belong to them.

The sun goes down; it gets darker. I must leave. Ancient laws, instinctual in our skin and tissues, let us know that it is not right to sit in the place where the dead are buried after the light disappears. Ancient stories remind us that there is a time to let go of our loved ones but carry their spirit with us.

And what is a place anyhow? We are from bodies, from land and landscape—they shape us and accompany us. When I leave this particular place, I will be accompanied home down the road by the current of energy I exchanged at these stones marking the places my family members entered the earth.

When I go to my hotel, I will enter a darkened room— will place my finger on the plastic switch that once I flip will draw a current of fire to the lamps, a current drawn from far in the north, from the river's current that rushes onward toward the bay.

I close my eyes and place my palms, one on each gravestone, and I think back to the moment in the sweat lodge when I heard my grandfather's voice. I think of Cross Lake and its people, its green towering trees, its murky lakes. And I remember the town of my childhood, now gone, just a forested field. I think of the young boy at Lee Roy's house, telling me, with eyes wide and earnest, *You're plugged in.* I hear the voice of the mothers calling out to me, *You've come back at last! We've been waiting for you.* My crane drifts somewhere in the depths of the lake.

What will I say now when I am asked, "Where are you from?" or "Where is home?"

Where am I from? I was born in England to parents who had crossed oceans from India to get there. We crossed other oceans to come to the middle of this continent, to the place the Red River and the Assiniboine River meet and mix their waters.

And then we went further north, decades now ago, to a place where the river lies across the lake, called from time beyond memory Pimicikamak.

It was there, at the shore of Kichi Sipi, near a place called Jane-nîpîy, where I first looked up into the night and learned myths and stories. It was there that I recited for the first time the earth's and sky's and water's many names.

Epilogue

CREE LANGUAGE AND culture classes flourish at the Mikisew School, and Cree Elders now come to the school to offer lessons in traditional arts and crafts such as storytelling, beading, weaving, making moccasins and fur-lined gloves as well as other kinds of leatherwork, and traditional drum and dance.

Chief Cathy Merrick did not win her re-election bid; Tommy Monias became Chief after her, and the current Chief is David Monias.

As of early 2020, construction has not yet begun on the promised hospital. Pimicikamak Okimawin continue their advocacy for the project with the provincial and federal governments and with Manitoba Hydro.

The government of Canada approved construction of Line 3, a new double-capacity pipeline running from the oil fields of Alberta to Lake Superior over the objections of First Nations communities in Alberta, Saskatchewan, and Manitoba, through whose territories the pipeline would run. As of this writing, construction is still held up by the State of Minnesota, which has not yet approved.

Acknowledgments

Excerpts from this book have appeared in *Bomb, Ecotone,* and *Georgia Review.* This book follows the style principles outlined in *Elements of Indigenous Style* by Gregory Younging (Brush Education, 2018).

I recounted the beginnings of my remembrances of Jenpeg and my initial contact with Cathy Merrick in my book *Silver Road: Essays, Maps & Calligraphies* (Tupelo Press, 2018). Some material from the opening chapter was adapted from that book.

Gratitude to Oberlin College for granting me research status during the 2016–2017 academic year, enabling my first trip to Pimicikamak and the research I conducted after. In particular I am grateful to Deans Tim Elgren, David Kamitsuka, and Eric Estes for their support. My local family—Marco, Irma, Genji, Minu, and Wiley—and friends, in particular Greggor Mattson, Jesse Keating, Nancy Boutilier, Christa Champion, Janet Fiskio, Ted Toadvine, Corinne Teed, Abbey Chung, Ben Jones, and Tanya Rosen-Jones, all held me in community.

I am ever grateful to Layli Long Soldier for the many gifts of her friendship over the years.

Critical to the writing of the first draft was the support of Alan Michael Parker and my appointment by Davidson College to the McGee Visiting Professorship in Creative Writing during the fall 2017 semester. I am especially grateful to Shireen Campbell and Kathy Barton of the English Department at Davidson for their support. Much of the first draft was written in the faculty writing group that took place at Sarah Luna's house. Thank you to my writing partners in that group and to Sarah for holding the space for us. Linda

Wu was my energetic and devoted research assistant during my time at Davidson, helping me find treaties, maps, and statistics, and to learn as much as I could about the technology of hydroelectricity.

I am grateful to my students and colleagues at the University of California San Diego for their interest and support of this work.

As a writer, I have been blessed to work with many wonderful editors and this project is no exception. Much gratitude to Daniel Slager and the staff at Milkweed Editions, who have been such champions, and to Susanne and Alan and all the staff of Goose Lane Editions who will publish a simultaneous Canadian edition. Jim Schley, who was my editor for *Silver Road*, also edited this work; his attentions humble me. Rhonda Kronyk made an immeasurable contribution in the final revisions, ensuring that the book spoke all the truth it needed to in the world. Jim and Rhonda, my deep thanks.

Countless gratitudes to the people of Pimicikamak who opened their hearts and homes to me. Many are named in this book, but in particular I thank Cathy Merrick, Lee Roy Muswaggon and his family, Jackson Osborne, Darrell Settee, Anna McKay, and Margaret Scott.

I am keenly aware of the long and sometimes problematic history of non-Indigenous people writing about Indigenous Peoples. I can only hope that the next book written about Cross Lake will come from the people of Pimicikamak, in particular from the young people, and it is my intention to do what I can to help this come to pass.

Finally, I have two questions that I hope the reader who has come this far will try to answer: Where does your electricity come from? Upon whose land does your home sit?

Notes

Chapter 1

8   Cathy Merrick, "Why We've Taken Back Jenpeg," *Winnipeg Free Press*, October 23, 2014, https://www.winnipegfreepress.com/opinion/analysis/why-weve-taken-back-jenpeg-280281072.html.

10   *The Final Report of the Truth and Reconciliation Commission of Canada. Vol. 1. Canada's Residential Schools* (Montreal and Kingston, McGill-Queen's University Press, 2015), 53.

12   Margaret Anne Lindsay and Jennifer S.H. Brown, *The History of the Pimicikamak People to the Treaty Five Period* (Winnipeg, Manitoba: The Centre for Rupert's Land Studies at The University of Winnipeg, 2008).

13   Bob Joseph, *21 Things You May Not Know About the Indian Act: Helping Canadians Make Reconciliation with Indigenous Peoples a Reality* (Port Coquitlam, BC: Indigenous Relations Press, 2018).

15   Noni E. McDonald, Richard Stanwick, and Andrew Lynk, "Canada's Shameful History of Nutrition Research On Residential School Children: The Need For Strong Medical Ethics in Aboriginal Health Research," *Paediatric Child Health* 19, no. 2 (February 2014), https://www.ncbi.nlm.nih.gov/pmc/articles/PMC3941673/.

16   Colin Gillespie, *Portrait of a People: A Study in Survival* (Winnipeg: Big Fizz, 2017).

17   Tanya Talaga, *All Our Relations: Finding the Path Forward*,
        CBC/Massey Lectures (Toronto: House of Anansi Press,
        2018).

Chapter 3

34   Micah Zerbe, "Food Insecurity in Manitoba: A Case Study of
        Cross Lake," *Universitas Forum: An International Journal on
        Human Development and International Cooperation* 5, no. 1
        (2016), http://www.universitasforum.org/index.php/ojs/article
        /view/198/645.

Chapter 4

39   Gary Mason, "The Suicide Epidemic of Cross Lake: Consider
        Urban Resettlement," *Globe and Mail* (Toronto), March 18,
        2016, updated May 16, 2018, https://www.theglobeandmail
        .com/opinion/behind-the-tragedy-of-cross-lake/article29282579.

40   Tracy Bear, "Impact of City Life," in *Indigenous Canada*
        MOOC, Tracy Bear and Paul Gareau, University of Alberta.
        https://www.coursera.org/lecture/indigenous-canada
        /impact-of-city-life-3oYTt.

Chapter 5

46   Harold Cardinal, *The Unjust Society* (Vancouver: Douglas &
        McIntyre, 1999).

46   Chelsea Vowel, *Indigenous Writes: A Guide to First Nations,
        Métis and Inuit Issues in Canada* (Winnipeg: Highwater
        Press, 2016).

46   Marcia Nickerson, "Characteristics of a Nation to Nation Relationship," Discussion Paper submitted to the Institute on Goverance, February 2017. https://iog.ca/docs/IOG-Nation-to -Nation-Discussion-Paper-2017-02.pdf.

47   Audrea Lim, "Has Trudeau (Politely) Betrayed Native People Again?" *The New York Times*, March 10, 2020. https://www .nytimes.com/2020/03/10/opinion/canada-natives-pipeline .html.

Chapter 7

61   CTV News, "Unmarked graves of children from residential school found beneath RV park," Friday, August 18, 2018. https://www.ctvnews.ca/canada/unmarked-graves-of-children -from-residential-school-found-beneath-rv-park-1.4076698.

61   Jen Skerritt, "Lost, but not forgotten: Push on to iden- tify graves of long-ago TB victims," *Winnipeg Free Press*, November 4, 2009. https://www.winnipegfreepress.com/local /lost-but-not-forgotten-69068562.html.

64   Johanna Theroux, "Characterising Turbidity and Identifying Sediment Sources in Norway House Cree Nation Drinking Water Using Sediment Fingerprinting," Master's thesis, University of Winnipeg, 2017, Annemieke Farenhorst and David Lobb, advisors, https://mspace.lib.umanitoba.ca /bitstream/handle/1993/32468/Theroux%20Johanna.pdf.

65   Lake Winnipeg Regulation Project, Manitoba Hydro, https://www.hydro.mb.ca/corporate/facilities/water_levels /lake_winnipeg_regulation.

66   "The Northern Flood Agreement: Agreement between Her Majesty the Queen in Right of the Province of Manitoba, of

the First Part; and the Manitoba Hydro-Electric Board, of the Second Part; and The Northern Flood Committee, Inc., of the Third Part; and Her Majesty the Queen in Right of Canada as Represented by the Minister of Indian Affairs and Northern Development, of the Fourth Part", December 16, 1977, https://www.hydro.mb.ca/community/indigenous _relations/pdf/northern-flood-agreement-1977.pdf.

66   Glenn Sigurdson, *Vikings on a Prairie Ocean: The Saga of a Lake, a People, a Family and a Man* (Winnipeg, Manitoba: Great Plains Publications, 2014), 243.

67   Brian Grover, *Summer of '64 on the Nelson River: Planning Northern Projects for Southern Beneficiaries* (Manitoba Historical Society, 2017), PDF e-book, http://www.mhs.mb.ca /docs/memoirs/grover.pdf.

67   Clean Energy Commission, Hydroelectric Development in Northern Manitoba: A History of the Development of the Churchill, Burntwood, and Nelson Rivers, 1960-2015," 2016. (38). http://www.cecmanitoba.ca/cecm/hearings /pubs/Regional_Cumulative_Effects_Assessment /BackgroundInformation/Hydroelectric_Development_in _Northern_Manitoba.pdf.

68   Danton Unger, "Lake St. Martin First Nation residents still waiting to go home after nine years," CTV News, January 16, 2020. https://winnipeg.ctvnews.ca/lake-st -martin-first-nation-residents-still-waiting-to-go-home-after -nine-years-1.4771389.

69   Austin Grabish, "Death toll in flooded-out Manitoba First Nation hits 92 as evacuees wait to return home," CBC News, April 17, 2017, https://www.cbc.ca/news/canada/manitoba /death-toll-in-flooded-out-manitoba-first-nation-hits-92-as -evacuees-wait-to-return-home-1.4040365.

69   Laura Reston, "The Forgotten First Nation," *The New Republic*, June 18, 2017, https://newrepublic.com /article/142461/forgotten-first-nation-floods-canada-homeless.

Chapter 8

72   Gavin Fisher, "BC Hydro Acknowledges Dark History of W.A.C. Bennett Dam in New Exhibit," CBC News, June 15, 2016. https://www.cbc.ca/news/canada/british-columbia/bc -hydro-acknowledges-dark-past-of-wac-bennett-dam-1.3637489.

73   John Woods, "Manitoba Premier Apologizes to First Nation for Damage Done by Dam," *Globe and Mail* (Toronto), January 20, 2015, https://www.theglobeandmail.com/news /national/manitoba-premier-apologizes-to-first-nation-for -damage-done-by-dam/article22541829.

74   Bruce Owen, "Schreyer says NDP bungling Hydro: Warns rates will soar due to new projects," *Winnipeg Free Press*, July 18, 2015, https://www.winnipegfreepress.com/local /schreyer-says-ndp-bungling-hydro-316650971.html.

74   "Pimicikamak Elder Weighs in on Manitoba Premier's Hydro Apology," CBC News, January, 21, 2015, http:// www.cbc.ca/news/canada/manitoba/pimicikamak-elder -weighs-in-on-manitoba-premier-s-hydro-apology-1.2927127.

76   Ryan Flanagan, "Cross Lake Community Council signs settlement agreement with province and Manitoba Hydro," *Thompson Citizen*, September 24, 2010. https://www .thompsoncitizen.net/news/nickel-belt/cross-lake-community -council-signs-settlement-agreement-with-province-and -manitoba-hydro-1.1367527.

78   "Jordan's Principle Implementation Act," Legislative Assembly of Manitoba, Bill 203, Third Session, Thirty-Ninth Legislature,

2009, https://web2.gov.mb.ca/bills/39-3/b203e.php or (bilingual) https://web2.gov.mb.ca/bills/39-3/pdf/b203.pdf.

78   United Food and Commercial Workers Action Center, "Help support justice for First Nations children," http://www.ufcw.ca/index.php?option=com_content&view =article&id=32521&Itemid=2345&lang=en.

78   "Alberta government signs Jordan Principle agreement with feds, First Nations Group," GlobalNews.ca, November 16, 2018, https://country105.com/news/4669767/alberta-jordans -principle-feds-and-first-nations.

87   Rodolfo Stavenhagen, "Report of the Special Rapporteur on the situation of human rights and fundamental freedoms of indigenous people," Economic and Social Council, United Nations, January 26, 2004. http://daccess-ods.un.org /access.nsf/Get?Open&DS=A/59/258&Lang=E. See also https://www.un.org/press/en/2004/hrcn1079.doc.htm.

95   Will Gilmore, Gilmore Cultural Resources Management Consulting, public testimony on Heritage Resources Inventory and Impact Assessment for the Wuskwatim Projects, Manitoba Clean Environment Commission, April 8, 2004. https://webcache.googleusercontent.com/search?q =cache:gyMZuqaPPNIJ:www.cecmanitoba.ca/resource /hearings/37/apr0804.txt+&cd=1&hl=en&ct=clnk&gl=us. See also https://www.ncncree.com/business-and-economy /wuskwatim-project.

Chapter 11

107   Zebedee Nungak. *Wrestling with Colonialism on Steroids: Quebec Inuit Fight for Their Homeland.* (Montreal: Véhicule Press, 2017).

107   Evelyn J. Peters, "Native People and the Environmental
       Regime in the James Bay and Northern Quebec Agreement,"
       Arctic Vol. 52. No. 4 (December 1999): 395-410.

120   Harold Johnson, *Firewater: How Alcohol Is Killing My
       People (and Yours)* (Regina, Saskatchewan: University of
       Regina Press, 2016).

Chapter 15

160   Gossan Resources, Ltd., "Statement on Pipeline Lake Project for
       Titanium, Vanadium, and Iron Mining in Cross Lake," http://
       www.gossan.ca/projects/pipestone.html.

160   Clean Environment Commission of Manitoba, "Review of
       Regional Cumulative Effects Assessment," May 28, 2018,
       http://www.cecmanitoba.ca/cecm/hearings/rcea.html.

Epilogue

169   Jessica Botelho-Urbanski, "Cross Lake residents still waiting
       for health complex: Community hopes birthday card cam-
       paign will help sway health minister," June 18, 2018,
       https://www.winnipegfreepress.com/local/cross-lake-residents
       -still-waiting-for-health-complex-485836651.html.

169   Amelia Diehl, "On Indigenous Peoples Day Anishinaabeg
       Leaders March Against Enbridge's $7.5 Billion Oil Pipeline,"
       In These Times, October 14, 2019. https://inthesetimes.com
       /article/22116/indigenous-peoples-day-anishnabeeg-leaders
       -march-against-line-3-pipeline.

Suggestions for Further
Reading and Viewing

Archibald, Jo-ann, Jenny Lee-Morgan, and Jason De Santolo, eds. *Decolonizing Research: Indigenous Storywork as Methodology.* London: Zed Books, 2019.

Barker, George. *Forty Years a Chief.* Winnipeg: Peguis Press, 1979.

Beardy, Flora and Robert Coutts, eds. *Voices from Hudson Bay: Cree Stories from York Factory.* Rupert's Land Record Society Series. Montreal: McGill–Queen's University Press, 1996.

Burns, Devon. TSN Original, documentary video on baseball in Cross Lake: "The Sound of Thunder." https://vimeo .com/248790998 (trailer at: https://www.facebook.com/TSN /videos/10155048596971055/).

Crey, Ernie; and Suzanne Fournier. *Stolen From Our Embrace: The Abduction of First Nations Children and the Restoration of Aboriginal Communities.* Vancouver: D&M Publishers Inc, 1998.

Culver, Leah, co-dir. *Ininnewi Pimatisiwin: Land Use and Occupancy Study 2015.* Cross Lake, Manitoba: Pimicikamak Okimawin, 2015.

Daschuk, James W. *Clearing the Plains: Disease, Politics of Starvation, and the Loss of Indigenous Life.* Canadian Plains Studies Series. Regina, Saskatchewan: University of Regina Press, 2019.

Estes, Nick. *Our History is the Future: Standing Rock versus the Dakota Access Pipeline and the Long Tradition of Indigenous Resistance.* London, UK: Verso, 2019.

Fernando, Nixon. *The Tragedy of Farmers' Suicides in Vidarbha: A Lesson and a Ray of Hope*. New Delhi, India: Rupa and Co., 2009.

The Fifth Estate, CBC/Radio Canada: "Cross Lake: 'This Is Where I Live.'" Season 42, Season Finale. Broadcast date: April 7, 2017. https://www.cbc.ca/player/play/916557379620 or https://www.youtube.com/watch?v=xfPrfZfPhbY.

French, Alice. *My Name is Masak*. Winnipeg: Peguis Press, 1977.

Hubbard, Tasha, dir. *Birth of a Family*. Montreal: National Film Board of Canada, 2017. Film available at: https://www.nfb.ca/film/birth_of_a_family/.

———. *Two Worlds Colliding*. Montreal: National Film Board of Canada, 2004. Film available at: https://www.nfb.ca/film/two_worlds_colliding/.

Indigenous Corporate Training, Inc., *The Indian Act and the Pass System*, July 23, 2015. https://www.ictinc.ca/blog/indian-act-and-the-pass-system.

King, Lisa, Rose Gubele, and Joyce Rain Anderson, eds. *Survivance, Sovereignty, and Story: Teaching American Indian Rhetorics*. Boulder, Colorado: Utah State University Press, 2015.

King, Thomas. *The Truth About Stories: A Native Narrative*. CBC/Massey Lecture Series. Minneapolis: University of Minnesota Press, 2005.

McCutcheon, Sean. *Electric Rivers: The Story of the James Bay Project*. Montreal: Black Rose Books, 1991.

McLeod, Darrel J. *Mamaskatch: A Cree Coming of Age*. Minneapolis: Milkweed Editions, 2019.

McLeod, Neal. *Cree Narrative Memory: From Treaties to Contemporary Times.* Saskatoon, Saskatchewan: Purich Publishing, 2007.

Merasty, Joseph Augie, with David Carpenter. *The Education of Augie Merasty: A Residential School Memoir.* Regina, Saskatchewan: University of Regina Press, 2017.

Obomsawin, Alanis, dir. *Jordan River Anderson: The Messenger.* Montreal: National Film Board of Canada, 2019. Trailer at https://www.nfb.ca/film/jordan-river-anderson-the-messenger/.

———. *Our People Will Be Healed.* Montreal: National Film Board of Canada, 2017. Complete film at https://www.nfb.ca/film/our-people-will-be-healed/.

———. *We Can't Make the Same Mistake Twice.* Montreal: National Film Board of Canada, 2016. Complete film at https://www.nfb.ca/film/we_can_t_make_the_same_mistake_twice/.

Page, Ellen, and Ian Daniel, dirs. *There's Something in the Water.* Canada: 2 Weeks Notice Studio, 2019.

Purdon, Nick. *The National:* CBC News: "Manitoba teacher hopes goose hunting will help save his students: Six young people in Cross Lake committed suicide in three months." May 11, 2016, https://www.cbc.ca/news/indigenous/cross-lake-manitoba-kerry-muswagon-fights-youth-depression-1.3575900 or https://www.youtube.com/watch?v=pefc8gK5yjg.

Richardson, Boyce. Foreword by Winona LaDuke. *Strangers Devour the Land.* White River Junction, Vermont: Chelsea Green Publishing, 2008.

Salaita, Steven. *Inter/nationalism: Decolonizing Native America and Palestine.* Minneapolis: University of Minnesota Press, 2016.

Sandford, Robert William. *Quenching the Dragon: The Canada–China Water Crisis.* Victoria, British Columbia: Rocky Mountain Books, 2018.

Shiva, Vandana. *Stolen Harvest: The Hijacking of the Global Food Supply.* Cambridge, MA: South End Press, 2000.

Simpson, Leanne Betasamosake. *As We Have Always Done: Indigenous Freedom Through Radical Resistance.* Minneapolis: University of Minnesota Press, 2017.

TSN Original, documentary video on baseball in Cross Lake: "The Sound of Thunder." http://www.tsn.ca/video/tsn-original-the-sound-of-thunder~1042300 (trailer at: https://www.facebook.com/TSN/videos/10155048596971055/).

TSN Original, documentary video on National Hockey League player Brady Keeper. "A Kid From Nowhere." https://www.tsn.ca/video/tsn-original-a-kid-from-nowhere~1580673.

Vermette, Katherena. *River Woman.* Toronto: House of Anansi, 2018.

Waldron, Ingrid R.G. *There's Something in the Water: Environmental Racism in Indigenous and Black Communities.* Black Point, Nova Scotia: Fernwood Publishing, 2018.

Poet, editor, and prose writer Kazim Ali was born in the United Kingdom to Muslim parents of Indian, Iranian, and Egyptian descent. He was raised in the United States and Canada, including several years spent in northern Manitoba when his father was working as an electrical engineer on the Jenpeg hydroelectric dam.

"A rich and daring poetic voice" (*Library Journal*), Kazim Ali is the author of numerous volumes of poetry, fiction, essays, and cross-genre texts. His collections of poetry include *Sky Ward*, winner of the Ohioana Book Award in Poetry, *The Far Mosque*, winner of Alice James Books' New England/New York Award, and most recently, *The Voice of Sheila Chandra*. Among his books of essays and non-fiction are *Resident Alien: On Border-crossing and the Undocumented Divine* and the hybrid memoir *Silver Road: Essays, Maps & Calligraphies*, in which Ali was praised by *Publishers Weekly* for transforming "readers into his companions on his travels...and on an interior philosophical quest." An accomplished translator and editor of several anthologies and books of criticism, Ali is currently a professor in the Literature Department at the University of California, San Diego. The UC San Diego campus, the city of San Diego, and the US-Mexico border nearby all sit on the traditional lands of the Kumeyaay.

Author photo by Tanya Rosen-Jones

Interior design by Mary Austin Speaker

Typeset in Walbaum

Walbaum is a German Modern typeface created in the Didone
style invented by Justus Erich Walbaum (1768–1839), a type
designer who trained as a spice merchant, pastry cook and coin
cutter. Inspired by the work of Firmin Didot in France and
Giambattista Bodoni in Italy, Walbaum's design uses sharper
contrast between thick and thin strokes and a squareness to
the characters. Justus Walbaum's designs have been listed as
an influence on nineteenth-century sans-serif typefaces
such as Univers and Helvetica.